HUKA LODGE'S COOK BOOK

RECIPES BY GREG HEFFERNAN
PHOTOGRAPHS BY JOHN PETTITT

Published by Huka Lodge

ACKNOWLEDGEMENTS

As the owner of Huka Lodge I wish to personally thank and acknowledge the following people for their contribution to Huka Lodge's Cook Book: Greg Heffernan for his total commitment to this project, and the dedication of his time and energy in preparing and presenting these superb menus. I also wish to thank Greg's wife, Julie, for her level of support and understanding during all the stages of this book; John Pettitt for the outstanding quality of his photography; Donna Hoyle whose design work, overall co-ordination, and professionalism have been invaluable in the production of this book; Geoffrey Martin who wrote the essay "Around the Great Lake" with the craftsmanship and skill he applies to all our publishing; Christopher Stevens, Wine Master, who described the selection of wines that comprise our comprehensive wine list; Martin Keay who wrote about the magnificent gardens; Virginia Fisher for all her energy and enthusiasm — from beginning to end of this project.

Finally, to all our staff who have worked so hard to ensure the success of Huka Lodge's Cook Book, my heartfelt thanks.

Alexander van Heeren.

Published by Huka Lodge,
P.O. Box 6993, Auckland, New Zealand.
Distributed in New Zealand by
Hodder & Stoughton,
46 View Road, Glenfield, Auckland.
Distributed in Australia by
Simon & Schuster Australia,
20 Barcoo Street, East Roseville, NSW 2069.
Copyright © 1989 Huka Lodge:
Greg Heffernan (recipes) and
John Pettitt (photographs)
First published 1989
Reprinted 1993
ISBN 0-473-00774-6

Printed in Hong Kong.

PUBLISHING CO-ORDINATOR: Donna Hoyle
EDITORS: Julie Dalzell and Sue Brierley
ART DIRECTION AND STYLING: Donna Hoyle
PHOTOGRAPHY: John Pettitt
DINNERWARE FOR PHOTOGRAPHY: The Studio of Tableware
JACKET AND BOOK DESIGN: Donna Hoyle
FINISHED ARTWORK: P.R. Graphics
TYPESETTING: Comset, Auckland
SEPARATIONS AND PLATES: Rainbow Graphics.
PRINTING AND BINDING: Everbest Printing Co. Ltd.

CONTENTS

INTRODUCTION

During the course of my business travels I have visited almost every corner of the earth, yet the peace and tranquillity of Huka Lodge, on the banks of the Waikato River, took me by surprise. This led to my eventual purchase of Huka Lodge. In a world that is becoming increasingly hurried and impersonal, Huka Lodge represents the calming elements we all crave.

We have been told that the Lodge has a charismatic effect on guests the moment they arrive. Suddenly the trauma of travel, the pressure of business and responsibilities of domestic life seem to be left far behind. This is exactly the way we intend your arrival to be and, after the relaxation of pre-dinner drinks, truly memorable food and wine await.

The originality of our food will impress you. Not just its careful preparation or its delightful presentation, but the sheer lavishness of the ideas that inspired each course. International gourmets and epicures have said that the kitchen of Huka Lodge has taken some of the freshest and most natural food in the world and created a standard against which New Zealand cuisine can be measured.

I am pleased, for this has been our mission. For those of you who have been our guests, we are sure Huka Lodge's Cook Book will bring back many pleasant memories. If you have yet to visit us, our Cook Book serves as a window to the fine food and wine you will be served.

Many people have contributed to Huka Lodge's Cook Book. This, like the food at Huka Lodge, has been a labour of love.

Alexander van Heeren

Huka Lodge, nestled among the trees on the banks of the Waikato River.

AROUND THE GREAT LAKE

Lake Taupo lies at the very heart of New Zealand's North Island, more than three hundred metres above sea-level. The lake is guarded to the south by a trilogy of snow-capped mountains and to the north, beyond rolling hills and vast, fragrant pine forests, are the geysers and fumaroles of the Rotorua thermal area.

Your first impression of Lake Taupo will be one of peaceful beauty. You will have been deceived because the origins of the lake are violent.

Little more than two thousand years ago an eruption of gigantic proportions took place. The explosions sent a shower of ash scattering for a radius of nearly one hundred miles.

The crater eventually began to fill with water and, according to the legend of the Maori people of the Tuwharetoa Tribe, Taupo Moana — the Sea of Taupo — was born. Filled by ice-cold rivers flowing from the mountains that rim the lake, Lake Taupo is crystal clear and breathtakingly cold.

At the northern tip a strong river leaves the lake on a three hundred kilometre journey to the sea. The Waikato is New Zealand's longest river. After a tortuous infancy, it thunders over a series of rapids that eventually become the Huka Falls. Their beauty will astound you, the deep aquamarine hue amaze you. These falls are nature at her theatrical best.

The Waikato River below the Lodge before cascading over the falls.　　　CRAIG POTTON

Huka Lodge shrouded in early morning mist.

Almost hidden in the trees above the falls is Huka Lodge, considered to occupy the most beautiful position of any lodge in the world. From here every nook and cranny of the Taupo region can be explored.

And there is much to do. The lake offers the best rainbow trout fishing in the world. For the skier, Mount Ruapehu has the longest runs on spring snow in the Southern Hemisphere. The mountains to the east provide hundreds of square kilometres of subalpine wilderness where deer and trout are the quarry of a dedicated fraternity of hunters and fishermen.

No matter what pursuit brings you to Taupo, you will do it in an environment that is pure and clean. You will be in a place where the air is so clear you can see for a hundred kilometres; where the seasons are so well defined as to appear carefully sketched.

Taupo's spring heralds the end of sharp winter snow winds, cracking frosts and runs of trout up tumbling rivers to spawn at their own place of birth. The summers are hot and the tussock of distant hills is parched by dry winds. Autumn? The leaf-change is so vivid that it sends splashes of gold running down the river valleys.

All this seems to happen in homage to the Great Lake.

ABOVE: From left, Mt Ruapehu, the cone of Mt Ngauruhoe and the flat peak of Mt Tongariro, seen from the Taupo township foreshore. BELOW: The Boat Harbour, Lake Taupo.

ONE OF THE WORLD'S SPECIAL PLACES

What is the magic of Huka Lodge? And why is it considered to be one of the greatest lodges of the world? The clue to the answer possibly lies in one word: uniqueness.

Since its formal restoration in 1985, Huka Lodge has enjoyed a renaissance which has once again given it world fame — something that tends to overshadow its simple beginnings when a young man first claimed its site by the edge of a remote Taupo river.

Alan Pye was a man whose eye could not conceal a glint. He led everyone to believe that he was Irish yet it has never been established. How he arrived in New Zealand or who first employed him also remains a mystery.

Pye's itinerant life changed when his love of fishing brought him to Taupo in the mid-twenties. In those days, Taupo was isolated and the journey from anywhere was regarded as a trek. Yet Taupo's fame as an angler's paradise was already established. Zane Grey had told the world of his massive catches on the Tongariro and already smaller lodges had begun to dot the lake's eastern shoreline.

Alan Pye, founder of Huka Lodge.

But it was the mighty Waikato that lured Pye. The river had a peerless reputation for its dry fly fishing. Each day, like clockwork, sedge fly would hatch from rafts of vivid green weed beneath the river's surface. Knowing that the river was popular with fly fishermen who were prepared to make the long trip, Pye decided to procure land on its banks and build a lodge.

The original Lodge, *circa* 1931.

The origins of Huka Lodge were humble, to say the least. Anglers were accommodated in huts with slatted floors. On each a stout wooden frame was draped with heavy canvas. Anglers slept here and joined Pye and his wife in the main lodge room for generous drinks and meals of ample proportion. Such was the Pyes' hospitality that the fame of Huka Lodge spread to every corner of the angling world. The quality of the fly fishing almost began to take second place to the conviviality and atmosphere the Lodge created.

By the mid-1930s, Pye's fame was at its peak. Flies had been tried and named after him. A New York angling club bore his name and the Lodge's visitors' book was silent testimony to its international reputation. The following names appeared: Her Royal Highness The Duchess of York, Charles E. Lindbergh, James A. Michener (who wrote part of *Return to Paradise* at the Lodge), as well as Governors-General and many famous film stars and politicians.

Things had never looked better for the Lodge. Then war came, and with it went the mobility of its international guests. At the same time, changes took place in the river itself. After the control gates were installed on the river at Taupo, water levels became too erratic for the delicate sedge and the fishing as a consequence diminished in value.

Of course, Pye's loyal patrons continued to come, but the emphasis moved to the lake and its rivers. This probably means that Pye could be called Taupo's first and foremost angling guide.

With advancing age, Pye's involvement decreased. He died in 1973 at Taupo, an international identity who will never be forgotten. Alan Pye's main legacy is that of personal hospitality and that is the cornerstone of the Lodge today.

Without doubt, the Lodge's location is unique in itself. Set in seven private hectares, with wide sweeps of lawn running up from the river, Huka Lodge is one of those few places that establishes its charm immediately with its guests. Redwoods tower above its wooden shingle roof and the very architecture of the Lodge suggests that it is at one with its environment. Now, instead of canvas-framed sleeping quarters, a series of lavish individual lodges house guests. Each lodge is nestled in native trees and faces directly on to the river.

The guest lodges at Huka Lodge.

It was not like this when the present owner, Alex van Heeren, bought the property. His goal was to recreate the ambience of the early days of the Lodge by gathering a group of individually talented people who were as motivated as he.

He needed an architect who could identify with the Lodge's past, present and future, to provide designs that would contribute to its unique character; builders who could translate design into reality — who saw materials as a medium of expression and whose craftsmanship would stand the test of time. He sought a landscape gardener to enrich the contours of these perfect hectares and to plant trees to enhance the already beautiful environment. He needed an interior designer who believed that any form of ostentation is distasteful.

Once he found his team, van Heeren told them of his expectations. They in turn expected much of him. They persuaded and cajoled until their ideas were accepted.

The result in terms of interior design is one of eclectic and ambient charm. The designer, Virginia Fisher, never lost sight of the fact that Huka Lodge is a country lodge. She skilfully combined antique Georgian country furniture imported from Europe with solid and comfortable pieces made locally.

The paintings at Huka Lodge are a delight to behold. Some are 17th Century European, some are local. Each work has been chosen for its fish or game theme. Scattered throughout the Lodge, sometimes in the most unexpected places, you will find the Lodge's discreet tartan motif.

Informed opinion describes the design of Huka Lodge as possessing a rare quality, that of understated taste executed with style and flair.

The main Lodge is the centre of activity. Here guests gather to dine, meet guides and, over pre-dinner drinks, regale each other with the events of the day: of river, lake, court and course.

The Lodge Room, where guests gather for pre-dinner drinks.

Staff members go out of their way to provide superb low-key service and ensure that guests enjoy their time at the Lodge. Never obtrusive, they make a point of arranging anything a guest requires. It may be fishing guides for fly angling on Taupo's rivers, a cruise on the Lodge's own high-speed vessel, *Prime Time,* to the Western Bays for a spot of armchair angling or a picnic, helicopter flights to the wilderness, horse trekking, a few rounds of golf on Wairakei's world-rated course or just a few fresh tennis balls for a couple of quick sets on the Lodge's own court.

Fly fishing for rainbow trout.

In an increasingly impersonal world, the service and aura of Huka Lodge remain the essence of its charm. Perhaps this is why the respected Relais et Châtcaux organisation awarded Huka Lodge its prestigious Yellow Shield, the only such award made in New Zealand. Its criteria? That a Lodge should offer the highest standards of character, courtesy, calm, comfort and cuisine.

This spirit of excellence has meant that the Lodge has found itself in a world spotlight on many occasions. Andrew Harper, the noted United States travel writer, said: "In a country not known for its epicurean cuisine, Huka Lodge reigns supreme." In Lord Lichfield's *Courvoisier's Book of the Best* appears the comment: "My favourite holiday place in the world is Huka Lodge in Taupo. It is equal to the best five star accommodation in the world."

Further international acclaim came when Huka Lodge was chosen as the venue for the 1987 GATT Conference on Tariffs and Trade. Ministers from 24 member nations spent two days at the Lodge for one of the most important conferences of its kind in recent years.

The Lodge has become the retreat of royalty and several crowned heads of European Houses have visited Huka Lodge for a brief sojourn in a round of hectic duties. Television crews have visited the Lodge to film sequences for such programmes as *Lifestyles of the Rich and Famous*.

Huka Lodge is now a tribute to the foresight of Alex van Heeren, the businessman who came here and saw the potential of the Lodge and its site. In the Queen's honours list of 1988, Alex van Heeren was made an Honorary Member of the Order of the British Empire for his services to tourism and exports. He divides his time between various business interests and his role as Honorary Consul of the Netherlands in Auckland.

Just as Alan Pye shaped the Lodge's past, Alex van Heeren plotted its future. Yet some things about Huka Lodge will never change. Its magic is ever-present. As present as the river mists that greet each guest every morning as if to remind them that this river will flow forever.

THE GARDENS

Compared to the uniform, yet bland good taste of international high-rise hotels with their panoramic scenery, Huka Lodge offers total seclusion and privacy in a dramatic setting only a few minutes from Taupo airport. The park-like ambience beside the swift-flowing Waikato River is part of a distinctively New Zealand experience.

Early photographs of the area show a largely barren and treeless landscape, but the gardens now benefit from a planting programme which showed great foresight. Mature pines, redwoods and firs now provide an established backdrop for the recently re-developed grounds. The river and a small stream set among sweeping shrubberies provide a perfect setting for a woodland and stream garden, extensive lawns being framed by drifts of flowering trees and shrubs. In the sheltered glades maples, magnolias, flowering cherries, azaleas and rhododendrons thrive in the perfect climate and the light soil. Growth is very rapid, though the mild climate means that plants have a shorter life than in comparable places overseas. An ongoing planting programme includes hundreds of trees such as Scots pines, beeches, firs and spruces together with native rimu and kauri so that the woodland quality of the gardens will always provide privacy and enclosure.

The water garden at the Lodge.

Spring and early summer are the peak seasons for colourful effects. Hundreds of daffodils appear under the trees, to be followed by early blossom and the unfolding of moisture-loving plants alongside the margins of the stream. Hostas with their bold foliage, astilbes, asiatic primulas and many different varieties of iris continue to provide colour and interest until Christmas, with weeping maples, spiraea and white hydrangeas on the banks. Colours tend to be white and yellow, with the blues and purples of the iris, while bright pinks and reds have been avoided. Rhododendrons and azaleas continue this restrained colour theme.

Summer interest is provided in the herbaceous planting above the ponds, with simple, old-fashioned flowers massed together — foxgloves, delphiniums, Queen Anne's lace, cosmos and larkspur, many providing cut flowers for the Lodge. Unfortunately, opossums have made the growing of roses impossible at the moment. Autumn colour is wonderful in Taupo, many plants showing gold and scarlet leaves over a period of many weeks. A whole bank in the garden is planted to create just these effects, displaying pyracanthas, rowans, and crabapples with their beautiful fruit as well. Eventually, a forest of beech trees will form a dramatic backdrop.

Another recent development has been a formal herb garden, planted close to the kitchens, and surrounded by a wisteria-covered pergola. Citrus does well in this sheltered corner, with bay trees, rosemary and a wide variety of culinary herbs enclosed within hedges of dwarf English lavender. The garden is both practical and decorative: for the chef, and for the guests to enjoy on their way to their rooms.

Apart from a restful setting and botanical interest, the grounds of the Huka Lodge provide for outdoor activities with a tennis court and a spa pool; an enclosed area has been specially designed for outdoor functions, while the main terrace gives a dramatic view of the river that the guests can admire while sitting and eating their luncheon. A summerhouse at the water's edge is the perfect setting for afternoon tea, or for an evening event when the lights illuminate the background trees. Birdlife thrives everywhere, their songs and the sound of the river being the only things to break the perfect stillness of the Huka Lodge gardens.

A drift of Iceland poppies.

THE WINES OF HUKA LODGE

A wine list is a simple thing to organise anywhere but in the climate of winemaking in New Zealand. This has got nothing to do with the actual weather but is because of the enormous changes that have taken place as New Zealand finds itself amongst the foremost of winemaking countries in the world.

When the first wine lists were prepared for Huka Lodge, it was fashionable for guests to buy French wine and German wine. After that Australia had but a brief reign before the realisation that New Zealand now had wines of which she could be proud internationally, and it was decided to make the list a mainly New Zealand showcase.

Easier said than done, for instead of three areas, Hawke's Bay, Gisborne and Auckland, there were two new areas, Marlborough and Nelson, which, by right, had to be included. Just when all that was getting settled, suddenly, over the hills from Wellington, another new area arrived in Martinborough.

There were then the wines from the satellite areas such as Waiheke Island and the wines of Canterbury. That may seem very simple until one realises that there are normally at least three or four vineyards in each *new* place that are worthy of being represented, and that in many of these areas the vineyards produce Chardonnay, Sauvignon Blanc, Rhine Riesling, Gewürztraminer, and the grape that many New Zealanders grew up on, Müller Thurgau, as well as the red varieties of Cabernet Sauvignon, Merlot, Cabernet Franc, Pinotage, and Pinot Noir. Add in Chenin Blanc and Semillon for the whites and the blends of red and one begins to see the problem. On top of that, New Zealand suddenly started to produce dessert wines and méthode champenoise.

It would be marvellous to accommodate all these wines but Huka Lodge, by its very exclusivity, is small and individual, and storage, while very adequate, is not unlimited, so it makes the choosing of the wines a very *delicat* task, as the French would say.

Of course, not everyone wants to drink New Zealand wine. Our guests come from all over the world, and they often want to try a little of the wine that they know from home. So, Australian wines are there but the list cannot include all those that deserve to be represented.

In addition, there are many American guests so the Lodge has included the keynote wines of California.

And then there is Europe! It would be unthinkable for so superb an establishment not to have the finest of the wines of Bordeaux and Burgundy. Château Haut Brion 1953 or Château Latour 1961 would seem perfect to accompany the most lucullan of dinners, and with at least 25 other clarets from the best châteaux of Bordeaux from which to choose, the Bordeaux selection is truly catholic. As to Burgundy, there is a small but carefully chosen list, and also some of the greatest quaffing wines of all from Beaujolais. Two delicious Sauvignons from the cradle of Sauvignon Blanc, Sancerre and Pouilly Fumé, are there for comparison with the best that Marlborough can offer, together with a

Riesling and Gewürztraminer from the classic area of Alsace.

When it comes to dessert wines, New Zealand makes quantum leaps each year, and what more perfect way to end a meal than a glass of sweet wine to accompany the superb temptations that are offered. For the grand finale, there is always a glass of the best from Portugal. And last, but in reality it should be first, is Champagne. Huka Lodge has its own label made by a very prestigious Grande Marque house in Ay, home of Champagne, as well as a full range of other Grande Marques.

There is always a small selection of wines of which there are too few to print on the wine list. A quiet word to the manager will reveal some jewels in the crown.

Salut!

AN INTRODUCTION TO THE RECIPES

We have compiled the following recipes in the form of a series of menus. These 20 menus comprise a collection of our favourites and all are typical of the food prepared and served at Huka Lodge. None have been created especially for this book. Our menus are a deliberate arrangement of flavours, textures, colours and, most importantly, taste. They typify the Huka Lodge style — honest food using the freshest of ingredients, originality, sound procedure and technique followed by superb presentation.

These recipes were originally developed by a chef for use in a professional kitchen. You will find that with very little adaptation on our part they have become suitable for your needs in a domestic kitchen.

Quantities in brackets (e.g. 25g [1oz]) are designed for American readers, therefore ounces, cups, pints have been used for larger quantities. American tablespoons are slightly different from ours so these have also been given. Conversions are to the nearest measurable equivalent, so in any cases where the exact measurement is vital, please check.

Read each recipe right through carefully prior to starting. Make sure you have all the ingredients required and all necessary equipment. Be sure you understand what is to be done; be organised and thorough, and nothing from the Huka Lodge Cook Book should be beyond your range.

The recipes and menus have been compiled with a sincere desire that anyone reading this book will find some, we hope many, points of interest, whether it be in a menu, an individual recipe, a style of presentation or a combination of ingredients. Our goals are to instruct, help and advise you and to share the great pleasures of food.

Cooking is fun and can provide great satisfaction for you and those you care about. Do not be discouraged by failures — I'm not. Use your culinary imagination — experiment and, most importantly, enjoy!

Greg Heffernan
Executive Chef

The preparation of this terrine is similar to that of a bavarois. Timing is essential. If the jelly is too warm, it will separate; if too cool, it will be impossible to work with. Therefore be well organised before you start.

Baby leeks, about the size of spring onions, are commonly available nowadays. Try to buy leeks that are evenly sized, with a long white section. If you cannot buy baby leeks, use regular leeks cut into strips. Blanch the leek first then cut it, otherwise the strips will disintegrate.

We use an enamel terrine mould for this recipe, one which will hold 1.2 litres (5 cups) of fluid. We find this type of terrine very useful as it can be used for the production of many different hot or cold pâtés and terrines. A very worthwhile piece of equipment in any kitchen.

INGREDIENTS — SERVES 15
TERRINE

14	baby leeks
100g (4 oz)	clean leek trimmings (use the lighter green pieces)
250g (9 oz)	raw turkey breast meat
100g (4 oz)	turkey trimmings
50ml (3½ tbsp)	olive oil
1	medium-sized onion, diced
2	parsley stalks
3	chervil stalks
700ml (3 cups)	Chicken or Turkey Stock (see page 138)
7–8	gelatine leaves or 20g or 6 level tsp (½ oz) gelatine powder
	white pepper and salt
1–2	egg whites
150ml (⅔ cup)	double cream

LEEK AND TURKEY TERRINE

METHOD: Trim the leeks to approximately 10cm (4″) lengths, reserving 100g (4 oz) of the trimmings. Blanch the leeks until soft; refresh. Trim the turkey breast, again reserving 100g (4 oz) of the trimmings. Slice the breasts into very thin escalopes. Quickly sauté on both sides in olive oil until golden and just cooked through. Dry with kitchen paper and allow to cool completely. Put aside until needed.

Finely chop the onion, leek trimmings and turkey trimmings. Lightly cook, without allowing to colour, in a pot with the herb stalks and 100ml (half a cup) of the chicken stock.

Soak the gelatine leaves in cold water until soft. Squeeze out and add to the trimmings. Alternatively, dissolve powdered gelatine in a little stock then add to the trimmings. Stir to ensure all the gelatine dissolves.

Add all the remaining stock to the pot. Remove from the heat, pour into a liquidiser and process until smooth. Pass through a fine sieve into a clean bowl, pushing through as much of the liquid and purée as possible. Season to taste. Place the jelly over ice or in a cool place, stirring regularly with a wooden spoon as it begins to set.

Meanwhile whisk the egg whites to soft peaks, and three-quarters whip the cream ready for use.

Let the jelly set to about the consistency of unbeaten egg white. Now you must work with speed. Remove the jelly from the ice and keep it at room temperature. Whisk in all the cream and carefully fold in the beaten egg whites with a large spoon. Pour one-third into the bottom of the 1.2-litre (5-cup) terrine and allow it to set just a little. Lay 7 of the blanched leeks along the length of the terrine, then evenly place half the turkey pieces. Cover with another third of the bavarois mixture and repeat the process with the remaining leek and turkey. Top up with final third. Allow to set in the refrigerator for at least 4 hours. If well covered, it will keep 1–2 days.

TOMATO VINAIGRETTE: Make a small incision in the tomatoes. Plunge them into boiling water for 5 seconds then place them straight into iced water. Remove the skin.

Cut the tomatoes into quarters and remove the seeds. Slice the flesh into thin strips lengthways and place it in the basic herb vinaigrette. Allow to rest at room temperature for at least 1 hour before use.

TO SERVE: A terrine such as this should never be served straight from the fridge as the full flavours are not fully appreciated if it is over-chilled.

Carefully release the terrine from the rim of the mould with your fingers, tilt it onto its side and slide a knife down one side to allow the air in. Tip upside down and turn out onto a cutting board. Lightly mark out your cutting points then slice while still firm with a very sharp, thin-bladed knife, or an electric knife. Place slices on the serving plates. Do this 20 minutes before you intend to serve the terrine so it has time to warm and soften very slightly. Dribble vinaigrette around each slice and garnish with a few small lettuce leaves. Serve immediately with toasted brioche or French bread.

TOMATO VINAIGRETTE

4	medium-sized tomatoes
600ml (2½ cups)	Huka Lodge Vinaigrette (see page 136)

CONSOMMÉ AND SAVOURY PARCELS

A consommé should be crystal clear. The clarification process is caused by the albumen in the egg white and the meat coagulating as they are heated, thus rising to the top of the liquid, carrying all other solid ingredients with them. The remaining liquid beneath the coagulated crust should be gently simmering.

Cloudiness could be due to poor quality or greasy stock, stirring after boiling point is reached, or lack of cleanliness of pots and cloth.

As this consommé was in our recent Christmas menu, the savoury parcel is the shape of a Christmas cracker or bonbon. This is just a variation of a ravioli; any shape may be used with any suitable filling.

This recipe may be halved or doubled quite safely according to the number of portions you require. Consommé kept in a sealed container in the refrigerator will keep 3–4 days. It can also be frozen in blocks very successfully.

INGREDIENTS — SERVES 15

CONSOMMÉ

4 litres	(7 pints)	Chicken Stock (good quality that gels when cold; see page 138)
500g	(1 lb)	raw, lean chicken meat, minced
100g	(4 oz)	leek, finely chopped
100g	(4 oz)	celery, finely chopped
50g	(2 oz)	carrot, finely chopped
50g	(2 oz)	onion, finely chopped
1 tsp		mixed herbs
1		medium-sized tomato, chopped
4		egg whites, whisked seasoning

GARNISH

50g	(2 oz)	thinly sliced carrot
50g	(2 oz)	thinly sliced leek
150g	(5 oz)	plain egg Noodle Dough (see page 137)
100g	(4 oz)	Savoury Farce (see page 136)
		a little beaten egg
		chives or strips of red pepper to tie parcels (optional)
		sprigs of fresh chervil

METHOD: Thoroughly mix 500ml (2 cups) of the cold chicken stock with all the other consommé ingredients. Add to the remaining stock in a heavy-bottomed pot.

Place over a gentle heat and slowly bring to the boil, stirring from time to time and making sure nothing is sticking to the bottom of the pot. Once at the boil, lower the heat so the consommé simmers very slowly. Do not stir or break the crust which has formed on the top. Simmer slowly for 1 hour without stirring.

GARNISH: Blanch the thinly sliced carrot and leek in a little boiling salted water. Refresh in iced water, strain and put aside.

Roll out the noodle dough very thin. If you have a pasta roller, roll it out on the thinnest setting. Leave the sheet of pasta to dry slightly on the bench top. Cut into 15 even rectangles approximately 9cm (4½″) long by 5cm (3″) wide. Place a teaspoon of savoury farce along the middle of each piece. Carefully brush around the farce with beaten egg then roll up. Tie each end with a piece of chive or red pepper, and press down all edges. Blanch in plenty of simmering salted water for 2–3 minutes. They will float when done. Once cooked, place the parcels in a bowl of cold water ready for use.

TO SERVE: Heat the consommé to serving temperature. Place a small bundle of julienne vegetables and 1 parcel (drained) in each hot soup bowl. Pour over the hot consommé, which will heat the garnish through. Float sprigs of chervil on each and serve immediately.

CHAMPAGNE AND STRAWBERRY SORBET

INGREDIENTS — SERVES 15

700ml	(3 cups)	water	juice of 2 limes or lemons
200g	(7 oz)	castor sugar	your favourite brut
700g	(1½ lb)	fresh ripe strawberries	champagne

METHOD: Add the sugar to the water and bring to the boil. Allow to cool. Hull the strawberries and purée with the lime or lemon juice in a liquidiser. Pass the purée through a fine sieve to remove the seeds etc.

Mix the purée into the cold sugar syrup and freeze right away, whisking from time to time. Alternatively, transfer it to a sorbetière and freeze.

If you are making a sorbet by hand, keep a close eye on it as it freezes, being sure to whisk it well so it freezes evenly and quite smoothly.

TO SERVE: Pipe or spoon the sorbet into elegant, small, long-stemmed glasses which have been chilled. Just before your guests are about to eat the sorbet pour over the chilled champagne.

SADDLE OF VENISON WITH CARAMELISED CHESTNUTS

METHOD: Add the red wine to the game stock, bring to the boil, skim and reduce by two-thirds over medium heat. Put aside. Season the venison with ground pepper and salt, and seal on all sides in the hot clarified butter, until evenly browned. Place in a preheated oven.

Venison is a very lean meat so I always cook it to medium-rare at 200°C (400°F). The cooking time will depend on whether you cut your meat into portions or leave it in larger pieces and slice it once done. Generally a good guide to follow is 15 minutes per 500g (1 lb) plus 20 minutes. Therefore 1kg (2 lb) would take approximately 45 minutes, although again this will depend on the cut you are using and your oven. Once cooked, allow to rest in a warm place for 10 minutes before you cut or serve it. This allows all the fierce heat to dissipate, so that the natural juices are not forced out of the meat when it is cut. It will also result in a more tender piece of venison.

METHOD: If using fresh chestnuts, score across the side of each nut with a sharp knife. Boil in plenty of water for 3–5 minutes, drain, then while still warm, peel off both the outer shell and the furry inner skin. Melt the redcurrant jelly in a flat sauté pan or frypan and add the venison jus. Add the chestnuts and over a steady heat reduce the liquid right down to a thick, sticky caramel consistency, tossing the chestnuts regularly and making sure they are well coated. Be careful not to overcook or reduce the liquid too far, or it will taste bitter. Keep warm until needed.

TO SERVE: Heat the jus to serving temperature, whisk in the knob of butter, and correct the seasoning. Slice the venison or place portions on hot plates and coat it in the game jus. Place the chestnuts on top. Garnish with fresh herbs and serve with seasonal vegetables tossed in Herb Butter (see page 132).

Farmed venison (deer meat) is widely available nowadays and strict laws of inspection and quality control are adhered to. Such venison has been killed at the best time to ensure good quality. If you are hunting the wild variety, then it is more a matter of pot luck. Venison should be hung in a cool, dry larder or stored in the refrigerator just chilled. Sprinkle it with ground ginger and pepper to keep the flies away.

Keep a very close eye on the ageing time, and examine the venison each day. At no time should it smell musty or off. Ageing can take from 10 days to 3 weeks, depending on the temperature. Always age the meat before you trim it ready for use; this saves wastage.

We generally use smaller red deer, as once aged correctly they have a nice game flavour. Fallow deer are very nice to eat but require much less ageing, and in our opinion have very little game flavour. As a general rule animals under 2 years taste the best; older is tougher.

INGREDIENTS — SERVES 15

1.2kg (2¾ lb)	venison (allow about 80g (3 oz) per person, free of all bones and sinew)

JUS

2 litres (3½ pints)	Brown Game Stock (see page 140)
300ml	red wine
	seasoning
	clarified butter
	knob of butter

Chestnuts may be bought ready shelled and cooked, although they can be a little expensive. If they are in season, they can be bought fresh and are easily prepared.

CARAMELISED CHESTNUTS

30–40	chestnuts (2–3 per person, depending on size)
1 tbsp	redcurrant jelly
200ml (1 cup)	venison jus

Good quality chocolate couverture is essential for this dish. Although dark, rich chocolate is generally used, a combination of dark and milk chocolate can also be delicious.

RUM AND RAISIN CHOCOLATE MOUSSE

INGREDIENTS — SERVES 15

CHOCOLATE MOUSSE

400g	(14 oz)	dark chocolate couverture
3–4		egg yolks
30ml	(2 tbsp)	dark rum
35g	(1½ oz)	castor sugar
125ml	(½ cup)	milk
100g	(3½ oz)	raisins
375g	(13 oz)	unsalted butter

CRÈME ANGLAISE

10		egg yolks
200g	(7 oz)	castor sugar
60ml	(4 tbsp)	brandy
900ml	(3¾ cups)	milk
1		vanilla pod (split)

METHOD: Melt the chocolate over a bain marie until it is smooth, with no lumps. Beat the egg yolks, rum and sugar together until the ribbon stage is reached. Bring the milk to the boil and pour it onto the yolks, whisking continuously. Pour the mixture back into the pan and set it over a low heat to cook.

Stir continuously with a wooden spoon, until the custard is thick enough to coat the back of the spoon. Do not allow the custard to boil. Strain and allow to cool.

Soak the raisins in warm water until they soften, then drain well and pat dry. Beat the butter until soft and creamy, then add to the cooled custard. Mix well into the melted chocolate; fold in the raisins. Pour into an enamel terrine or other suitable container and allow to set for a minimum of 4 hours.

CRÈME ANGLAISE: Place the egg yolks in a bowl and add the sugar and brandy. Whisk well until the ribbon stage is reached.

Pour the milk into a heavy-bottomed pot with the vanilla pod and bring to the boil. Pour the hot milk onto the egg mixture, whisking constantly. Pour the mixture back into the pot, set over a low heat and cook, stirring continuously with a wooden spoon, until the custard coats the back of the spoon. On no account allow the custard to boil.

Pass the custard through a fine sieve and allow it to cool completely. Stir from time to time so a skin doesn't form. Strain again, and cover with plastic wrap.

TO SERVE: Unmould the chocolate mousse by dipping the terrine in warm water and slowly easing the mousse out onto a cutting board. Slice with a sharp, thin-bladed knife into even portions, ready to serve. Pour a pool of crème anglaise into the middle of each cold plate and spread it out a little. Place a slice of chocolate mousse on top. Garnish with fresh fruit and berries and serve immediately.

SWEET PIMENTO BAVAROIS WITH A WALNUT AND HERB VINAIGRETTE

The overall success of this very delicate dish depends on the quality of the base stock. We use chicken stock, as its flavour complements that of the pimentos (peppers). A basic requirement is that the stock you use is concentrated enough to gel when cold. If it does not do this, we suggest reducing the stock over a steady heat to concentrate the flavour.

The basis of this recipe is a similar dish made by one of the Roux brothers. We have since developed it to suit our own taste and style. It is a savoury variation of the dessert bavarois; the principles and method are much the same.

METHOD: Cut the pimentos in half, remove the seeds and any white flesh. Roughly dice, keeping the colours separate. Cook each colour until tender in clarified butter, without allowing to colour, cooking the green pimento with the chopped herbs.

Soak the gelatine leaves in cold water, squeeze out, then add to the chicken stock. Warm the stock over gentle heat until the gelatine is totally dissolved. If using aspic powder, mix to a paste with stock or water then add to the warmed chicken stock.

Pass the stock through a fine sieve. Add one-third of the warm jelly to each colour pimento. Individually liquidise or blend each until smooth, then pass each into a clean bowl, pushing as much of the pulp through the fine sieve as possible. Season each colour to taste. Whip the egg whites to soft peaks, and two-thirds whip the cream. Put aside until needed. Place the yellow jelly over ice and stirring continuously allow it to set to the consistency of unbeaten egg white. Mix in one-third of the whipped cream, then carefully fold in one-third of the whisked egg whites.

One-third fill 6–8 x 100ml (½ cup) moulds with yellow bavarois. Allow to set firm in the refrigerator. Repeat this process, first with the red pimento, then with the green pimento, allowing each to set before the next colour is poured on top. Place in the refrigerator 3 hours before serving. To unmould, carefully place in warm water for an instant and turn out onto a chilled plate.

VINAIGRETTE: Place all the solid ingredients in a bowl. Add the juice and vinegar and mix together. Pour on the oils, whisking as you go. Correct seasoning. Allow to stand at room temperature for about 2 hours before serving.

TO SERVE: Place each bavarois in the centre of a serving plate, pour a cordon of vinaigrette around, and garnish with crisp salad leaves. Allow the bavarois to sit at room temperature for 20 minutes before serving, so the full flavour can be appreciated.

INGREDIENTS — SERVES 6–8

BAVAROIS

6		medium-sized pimentos, 2 red, 2 green and 2 yellow
30g	(1 oz)	clarified butter
1 tsp		chopped mixed herbs
4½		leaves gelatine or 15g (½–1 oz) aspic powder
350ml	(1½ cups)	strong Chicken Stock (see page 138)
		pepper and salt
1		egg white
75ml	(⅓ cup)	whipping cream

HERB AND WALNUT VINAIGRETTE

4		walnuts, finely chopped
1		shallot, finely diced
1		tsp wholegrain mustard
½		clove garlic, crushed
1 tbsp		fresh chopped mixed herbs
		salt and ground pepper
		juice of 1 lemon
3 tbsp	(4 tbsp)	white wine vinegar
100ml	(½ cup)	walnut oil
100ml	(½ cup)	salad oil

The mushrooms used in this consommé are not always easy to obtain, and they are also very expensive. However, the resulting soup is well worth the expense and effort. The mushrooms used are cèpe (a strong meaty fungus), chanterelle (a small, usually bright yellow mushroom with a delicate flavour), and regular cup mushrooms (those just past the button stage but not fully open). There is one other wild mushroom which we use more as a garnish, due to its enormous expense: the morel. One of the finest tasting mushrooms, it has a very rich, meaty flavour, and makes a memorable addition to any suitable dish.

The quenelles are optional and can easily be replaced by sliced mushroom, julienne vegetables or fresh herbs, or even a mixture of all these. However, the quenelles, small barrel-shaped mousses, do make a very interesting addition.

INGREDIENTS — SERVES 6

CONSOMMÉ

1500ml	(2½ pints)	strong Beef Stock (see page 140)
200g	(7 oz)	minced lean beef
50g	(2 oz)	cèpes (soaked in water for 30 mins if dried)
50g	(2 oz)	cup mushrooms
50g	(2 oz)	chanterelles (soaked in water for 20 mins if dried)
100g	(4 oz)	diced mixed vegetables (onion, carrot, leek, celery)
1		tomato, chopped
½ tbsp		chopped parsley
2–3		egg whites
		ground pepper and salt

SAVOURY QUENELLES

150g	(5 oz)	Huka Savoury Farce (see page 136)
15g	(½ oz)	finely diced morel
10g	(⅓ oz)	finely diced truffle (optional)

WILD MUSHROOM CONSOMMÉ

METHOD: Roughly chop all the mushrooms and thoroughly mix them together with the minced beef, vegetables, tomato and herbs. Add 250ml (1 cup) of the stock and mix well. Whisk the egg whites and beat into the mixture; season with freshly ground pepper and salt. Add to the remaining stock. Place over gentle heat in a heavy-bottomed pot and slowly bring to the boil. Stir from time to time, making sure nothing is sticking to the bottom. Once at the boil, lower the heat so the consommé simmers very slowly. Do not stir or break the crust which has formed. Simmer slowly for 1 hour.

Carefully strain the consommé through a fine sieve, lined with kitchen muslin or a damp teatowel, into a clean pot. Remove any fat that is floating on the surface with pieces of kitchen paper. Adjust the seasoning and put aside until needed.

GARNISH: Mix the finely diced morel and truffle with the savoury farce mixture. Bring salted water or chicken stock to the boil. Divide the quenelle mixture into 12 even portions, shape with 2 teaspoons into barrel shapes, and drop into the cooking liquid. Cook until they float, then remove from the heat and drain on kitchen paper.

TO SERVE: Heat the consommé to serving temperature. Place 2 quenelles in each hot soup bowl and pour over the soup. Sprinkle with chopped chives or picked chervil and serve immediately.

KIWIFRUIT AND BRANDY SORBET

When making this sorbet always try to use well-ripened kiwifruit. They are not only naturally sweeter but they pureé more easily.

INGREDIENTS — SERVES 6

350ml	(1½ cups)	water
90g	(3 oz)	sugar
500g	(1 lb)	ripe kiwifruit
30ml	(2 tbsp)	brandy
		juice of 1 lemon

METHOD: Add the sugar to the water and bring to the boil, simmer for 3 minutes. Allow to cool completely. Purée the peeled kiwifruit with the brandy and lemon juice. Pass through a fine sieve to remove the seeds etc.

Mix the cold syrup and purée together and freeze immediately, whisking from time to time to achieve a smooth and even finish. Alternatively, place in a sorbetière and freeze.

Pipe or spoon into glasses and garnish with a wedge of kiwifruit. Serve immediately.

VENISON MEDALLIONS

This is one of my favourite venison dishes, rich and gamy with the tangy bite of the onion confit.

The sauce is a slightly thickened glaze made from reducing stock and adding a little arrowroot to thicken and give it shine. We often use this glaze technique with beef stock as a base glaze for other meats, adjusting the flavour by infusing roasted bones and trimmings from the appropriate meat.

INGREDIENTS — SERVES 6

500g	(1 lb)	well-aged venison backstrip (approx. 80g (3 oz) per portion), free of all bone and sinew (other prime cuts may also be used) ground pepper and salt
50g	(2 oz)	clarified butter

ONION CONFIT

2		medium-sized onions, peeled
50ml	(3½ tbsp)	red wine vinegar
100ml	(½ cup)	grenadine ground pepper and salt

CHARTREUSE GLAZE

700ml	(3 cups)	Brown Game Stock (see page 140)
100ml	(½ cup)	red wine (burgundy if possible)
50ml	(3½ tbsp)	ruby port
1		level tbsp tomato paste
½ tsp		mixed dried herbs
50g	(2 oz)	mushroom trimmings
2g	(1 tsp)	arrowroot
30ml	(2 tbsp)	green chartreuse

VENISON: The trimmed meat may be sliced into 12 even medallions and sautéed, or left whole, browned on the stove top and finished in the oven. Whichever way you choose, season the meat well with freshly ground pepper and salt, then heat the clarified butter to a blue haze before adding the meat. Colour well on all sides and cook to medium rare. Rest the meat for 5 minutes in a warm place before you cut into it. If the meat is too hot, it will push out all the natural juices when cut.

ONION CONFIT: Cut the onions in half and thinly slice them across the grain. Add the red wine vinegar and grenadine to the onion. Place over steady heat and cook until the liquid has nearly all gone. Once reduced, season to taste and remove from the heat.

GLAZE: Add to the game stock the red wine, port, tomato paste, herbs and mushroom trimmings. Place in a heavy pot over a steady to high heat and reduce by two-thirds. Dilute the arrowroot with a little water then whisk it into the reduced glaze. Bring back to the boil, stirring all the time, and simmer for 3 minutes. Remove from the heat and pass through a fine sieve into a clean pot. Cover and put aside until needed.

TO SERVE: Heat the glaze to serving temperature, add the nip of chartreuse, and season to taste. A knob of butter whisked in at this stage adds a nice richness to the glaze. Warm the confit and evenly divide it between 6 hot plates. Slice or divide the meat into even portions and place over the confit, half covering it. Spoon the glaze over the meat and onion confit. Garnish with fresh herbs and serve immediately.

A nice vegetable accompaniment with this dish is Spinach Subric (a type of mousse; see page 130) and crisp baby vegetables tossed in Basil Butter (see page 132).

HAZELNUT AND FRANGELICO ICED SOUFFLÉ

This is a light, airy type of ice cream or iced parfait. The lightness is due to folding in the whisked egg whites just before freezing.

The soufflé may be served either as slices from a block or as individual portions poured into small ramekins with raised sides of tinfoil. When frozen, the foil sides are removed to give the puffed up soufflé effect. The high cream content makes it smooth and free of ice crystals once frozen. Well covered, it will keep some time frozen.

METHOD: Whisk the egg yolks, sugar and frangelico to the ribbon stage in a large bowl over a bain marie, making sure all the sugar is dissolved. The mixture should double in volume. Allow to cool, whisking regularly.

Roast the hazelnuts lightly under a grill until the skins begin to colour. Place in a bag and rub together to remove the brown skins. Finely chop or process in a blender; put aside.

Whip the cream until the whisk leaves tracks. Whisk the egg whites to soft peaks. Mix the hazelnuts into the cooled egg sabayon, then stir in the whipped cream, ensuring it is evenly mixed through. Finally, fold in the whisked egg whites carefully. Do not over-beat or bang the mixture at this stage or you will knock all the air out and lose the nice fluffy effect.

Pour into pre-prepared ramekins or any suitable container and freeze. We usually prepare the soufflé the night before so it has plenty of time to freeze.

CITRUS JUS: Remove the zest from the fruit with a zester or grater, place in a small pot with just enough water to cover, and add half a teaspoon of sugar. Reduce over steady heat until all the liquid has gone. Allow to cool.

Place the remainder of the sugar and the juice of all the fruit in a pot and bring to the boil. Dilute the arrowroot with a little water and whisk into the syrup. Simmer for 3 minutes. Pass through a fine sieve onto the zest, and mix together. Place in a clean bowl and allow to cool completely.

TO SERVE: Remove the iced soufflé from the freezer and allow it to soften just a little at room temperature. If slicing, flood a chilled plate with the citrus jus and place a slice on top. Garnish with some fresh lemon and orange wedges. Serve immediately. If serving from ramekins remove the tinfoil sides, garnish the top with fruit and whipped cream, and serve with an accompanying sauce boat of citrus jus.

INGREDIENTS — SERVES 6–8

5	egg yolks
110g (4 oz)	castor sugar
30ml (2 tbsp)	frangelico
50g (2 oz)	hazelnuts
300ml (1¼ cups)	double whipping cream
2	egg whites

JUS

	zest from 1 lime, 1 lemon and ½ an orange
50g (2 oz)	castor sugar
150ml (⅔ cup)	lemon juice
50ml (3½ tbsp)	lime juice
100ml (½ cup)	orange juice
2g (1 tsp)	arrowroot

GRAVLAX TARTARE

This dish is very simple to prepare, and very tasty. Gravlax is salmon marinated in dill, brown sugar, salt and oil for at least 24 hours. It is readily available in delicatessens and supermarkets and is generally of good quality. Unless you are familiar with a gravlax recipe, I would suggest you buy the ready-made product.

The caviar is not essential, and you can use ordinary hard-boiled eggs instead of quails' eggs. Just hard-boil an egg, allow it to cool, separate the white and yolk, then push each through a fine sieve. Place lines of each colour on top.

INGREDIENTS — SERVES 6

300g	(11 oz)	gravlax
30g	(1½ oz)	walnuts
		juice of 1 orange
		zest of ½ an orange, finely diced
1 dsp		walnut oil
1 tsp		chopped chives
1 tsp		chopped parsley
		seasoning
6		slices Brioche (see page 143)

GARNISH

6	poached quail eggs
3 tsp	caviar (optional)
6	sprigs dill
	crisp salad leaves
	Huka Lodge Vinaigrette (see page 136)

METHOD: Remove all the skin and bones from the gravlax. Cut it into thin strips, then finely dice, and place it in a clean bowl. Coarsely chop the walnuts and add them to the salmon. Finally add the orange juice, zest, walnut oil, chives, parsley and seasoning, and mix evenly into the salmon. Allow to rest for 1 hour before shaping.

Divide the salmon mixture into 6 even portions then press each portion in turn into a 5.5cm (2″) plain cutter to shape. Release onto a tray. Cover with plastic wrap and place in the refrigerator until needed.

Slice 6 pieces of brioche 1.5cm (½″) thick from a brioche loaf (see page 143). Cut with a 6cm (2″) plain cutter into discs. Place on a baking sheet and toast both sides under the grill. Put aside.

GARNISH: Bring a small pot of salted water to the boil. Carefully crack each quail egg shell with the back of a small knife, then cut through the membrane just under the shell. Drop the egg into boiling water and poach until just soft. Once done, place the eggs in cold water until needed.

TO SERVE: Place 1 salmon tartare on a disc of brioche in the middle of each plate. Place a quail's egg on top and spoon half a teaspoon of caviar over the egg. Finish with a small sprig of dill. Scatter small salad leaves around the edge of the plate then dribble herb vinaigrette over the leaves. Serve immediately with lots of accompanying warm brioche or toast.

DELICATE TOMATO AND BASIL CONSOMMÉ

Tomato and basil are meant for each other; the two flavours complement each other perfectly. This is a lovely consommé, delicate yet sharp, light yet satisfying.

METHOD: Roughly chop the basil and tomatoes, add them to the minced chicken, then mix in the diced vegetables and tomato paste. Lightly whisk the egg whites with 250ml (1 cup) of the cold chicken stock, then beat well into the chicken and vegetables. Season with ground pepper and salt. Add to the remaining stock and mix together in a heavy-bottomed pot.

Place over a gentle heat and slowly bring to the boil, stirring from time to time and making sure nothing sticks to the bottom. Once at the boil, lower the heat immediately so the consommé is just simmering under the crust which has formed. Do not stir. Simmer slowly for half an hour. Once cooked, carefully strain the consommé into a clean pot through a fine sieve lined with a kitchen cloth. Remove any fat from the surface with kitchen paper. Adjust the seasoning and put aside until needed.

GARNISH: Make a small incision in the tomato skin, plunge the tomatoes into boiling water for 5 seconds then straight into iced water. Remove the skin. Cut into quarters and remove all seeds. Slice the flesh into thin strips. Roll the basil leaves up and julienne.

TO SERVE: Heat the consommé to serving temperature. Place a little tomato and basil in each hot soup bowl and pour over the hot consommé. Serve immediately.

INGREDIENTS — SERVES 6

1500ml	(2½ pints)	Chicken Stock (see page 138)
200g	(7 oz)	lean chicken meat, minced
6		leaves fresh basil
3		soft tomatoes
100g	(4 oz)	diced mixed vegetables (onion, carrot, leek, celery)
75g	(3 oz)	tomato paste
2–3		egg whites
		ground pepper and salt

GARNISH

2	medium-sized tomatoes
1	bunch basil leaves

YELLOW TAMARILLO SORBET

Yellow tamarillos taste very similar to their red counterparts, but are possibly slightly less acidic. They make a very creamy smooth sorbet which is most refreshing.

INGREDIENTS — SERVES 6

350ml	(1½ cups)	water
100g	(4 oz)	castor sugar
3		ripe yellow tamarillos
		juice of 1 lemon

METHOD: Add the sugar to the water and bring it to the boil. Allow to cool completely.

Pour boiling water over the tamarillos and soak for 3 minutes, then plunge them into iced water. With a small, sharp knife peel off all the skin. Purée the tamarillos with the lemon juice then pass through a fine sieve into a clean bowl. Once the sugar syrup has completely cooled, pour it into the purée and mix together.

Freeze immediately, whisking from time to time to achieve a smooth and even finish. Alternatively place in a sorbetière and freeze.

TO SERVE: Pipe or spoon into chilled glasses and garnish with a sprig of fresh mint. Serve immediately.

TOURNEDOS OF BEEF

Tournedos are small, quite thick slices of fillet or tenderloin weighing 75–100g (3–4 oz). The cut is trimmed, tied to hold its shape and sautéed or grilled. There are some 250 classical ways of serving beef tournedos — the following dish is not one of them!

METHOD: Prepare and cook the egg noodles according to the basic recipe (see page 137). Refresh in cold water. Drain, and put aside until needed.

Peel the carrots then slice them very thinly lengthways. Trim the sides of each slice so they are even, then cut the carrot into strips the same width as the noodles.

Leaving the skin on the courgettes repeat the above process, making sure plenty of the strips have skin on them, as this is important for presentation. Blanch the carrots in plenty of boiling salted water until they are just soft and flexible. Do not overcook. Plunge them into iced water to halt the cooking process and enhance the colour. Blanch the courgette strips in the same water. They will only take 20–30 seconds to become crisp yet flexible. Plunge them straight into iced water. Put aside until needed.

Season each tournedos with ground pepper and salt and sauté in clarified butter until well browned on all sides. Place in a hot oven and cook at 200° C (400° F) for approximately 10 minutes. Remove from the heat and allow to rest in a warm place for a further 10–15 minutes.

Pour off any excess fat from the pan and add the madeira to take advantage of the flavours in the sediment remaining in the pan. Add the shallots and beef stock and reduce by half. Once reduced, pass through a fine sieve into a clean pot. Add the wholegrain mustard and cream. Slowly simmer until the sauce begins to thicken. The consistency should be such that it just coats the back of a spoon.

Thoroughly drain the vegetables and egg noodles and carefully mix them together. Reheat in a covered tray with a little butter and stock in a hot oven.

Sprinkle the noodles with chopped parsley and season.

TO SERVE: Heat the sauce to serving temperature, season to taste and whisk in a knob of butter. Make a nest of noodles on each of 6 plates. Place a tournedos in the middle of each. Pour the sauce over the meat and noodles and serve immediately.

INGREDIENTS — SERVES 6

6 x 100g (4 oz)	tournedos of beef
250g (9 oz)	plain Egg Noodles (see page 137)
4	medium-sized carrots
3	small, firm, yellow courgettes
3	small, firm, green courgettes
	ground pepper and salt
	clarified butter
1 tsp	chopped parsley

MUSTARD SEED SAUCE

100ml (⅓–½ cup)	madeira
50g (2 oz)	finely chopped shallots
600ml (2½ cups)	Beef Stock (see page 140)
1 tbsp	wholegrain mustard
125ml (½ cup)	cream
	seasoning
	knob of unsalted butter

Although we sometimes make individual fruit terrines, the best and easiest method is to make one in a standard 1.2-litre (5-cup) terrine mould. Serve one slice per person and present it as illustrated. Our standard recipe serves up to 15 people, depending on how generous you are.

Left in the mould, the fruit terrine will keep for several days; once turned out, if well covered, it will also keep 2–3 days. However, any leftovers are usually eaten the next day. This is a light, very refreshing dessert, delicious to eat.

Any fruit and berry variations may be used. These are my favourite combinations.

FRUIT AND BERRIES IN A CHAMPAGNE AND ORANGE JELLY

INGREDIENTS —
SERVES ABOUT 15

375ml	(1⅔ cups)	brut champagne
325ml	(1½ cups)	fresh orange juice
50g	(2 oz)	castor sugar
7		gelatine leaves or 20g (1 oz) powdered gelatine
18		large
or 27		medium-sized strawberries, hulled and trimmed
200g	(7 oz)	raspberries
25		green grapes, cut in half, seeds removed
25		black grapes, cut in half, seeds removed

RASPBERRY SAUCE

200g	(7 oz)	raspberries
400ml	(1¾ cups)	Sugar Syrup (see page 146)
		juice of 1 lime

METHOD: Chill a terrine mould. Mix the champagne, orange juice and sugar together in a pot. Soak the gelatine leaves in cold water until soft, then squeeze out. Add them to the champagne mixture. Place over a gentle heat to dissolve the sugar and gelatine. Pass through a fine sieve into a clean bowl and place over ice to cool.

Pour 100ml (½ cup) of the jelly into the bottom of the mould. Once firm, evenly lay the strawberries along the length of the mould, pointed end up. Add more jelly, just to the top of the strawberries, and set. Mix the grapes and raspberries together, sprinkle evenly along the length of the terrine, and top up with the remaining jelly. Set in the refrigerator for 2 hours before use.

SAUCE: Place the raspberries in a food processor. Process until smooth, adding sugar syrup as you go.

Pass through a fine sieve into a clean bowl to remove seeds etc. Add the lime juice. Cover with plastic wrap and store in the refrigerator until needed.

TO SERVE: Carefully release the jelly from the rim of the terrine. Place the terrine in warm water for the count of 10. Remove from the water, turn the terrine on its side and slide a flat knife or palette knife down the side to release the fruit terrine from the mould. Turn upside down and ease out onto your cutting surface. Mark out the cutting points and slice with a warm, sharp knife or electric knife. Place on chilled plates and spoon the raspberry sauce around. Garnish with fresh mint and enjoy with a glass of fine Sauternes.

PUMPKIN AND GINGER POTAGE

METHOD: Quickly sauté the onion and garlic in butter; do not colour. Add all the remaining ingredients except the cream, pepper and salt.

Slowly simmer until the pumpkin is soft, skimming off any impurities as they rise. Once cooked, cool a little, place in a liquidiser and process until very smooth.

Return to a clean pot and season to taste. Bring back to boiling point then add the cream just before serving. Do not boil once the cream has been added.

TO SERVE: Pour into 6 hot soup bowls and sprinkle with plenty of chopped chives.

INGREDIENTS – SERVES 6

1		small onion, diced
1		clove garlic, crushed
250g	(9 oz)	crown pumpkin, peeled and diced
25g	(1 oz)	butter
pinch		nutmeg
pinch		cinnamon
1 tsp		tomato paste
10g	(½ oz)	fresh ginger root, peeled and sliced
600ml	(2½ cups)	Chicken Stock (see page 138)
2		sage leaves freshly ground pepper and salt
100ml	(½ cup)	cream

In 1987 and 1988 I was a member of the National New Zealand Master Chefs Culinary Team competing in national and international Salons Culinaires.

To become a member of this team one had to compete in provincial and national cooking competitions, until the final five chefs were selected.

The following recipe is a slight variation of the seafood dish which played a large part in securing my selection for the team. Understandably I have quite a soft spot for it.

ROCK LOBSTER MEDALLIONS

INGREDIENTS — SERVES 6

3	rock lobster tails from 500–600g (1lb) lobsters
	ground pepper and salt
	butter

MOUSSE

6		whole scallops
100g	(4 oz)	orange roughy (deep sea perch)
75g	(3 oz)	salmon
2		cleaned and trimmed mussels
2		egg whites
30ml	(2 tbsp)	noilly prat
		juice of 1 lemon
200ml	(1 cup)	cream
		seasoning
25g	(1 oz)	butter

METHOD: Remove the rock lobster tails from the bodies. Retain the bodies and freeze for later use in soup or sauces. Shell and clean the meat, leaving the tails whole. Season with salt and ground pepper.

Brush 6 pieces of tinfoil with butter and wrap each tail, twisting the ends so a firm cylinder is formed. Put aside.

MOUSSE: Trim the roe from the scallops and reserve until the mousse is assembled. Ensure all the fish is free of bones and skin. Blend all the fish except the roe in a food processor until smooth, adding the egg whites and noilly prat as you go. Once this is done, push the mixture through a fine sieve into a clean bowl. This is quite difficult but is essential to ensure all pieces of sinew, bone, etc. are totally removed. Use a plastic scraper or the back of a ladle to push the fish through.

Place the bowl over a larger bowl of ice to keep it cold; this reduces the possibility of the fish purée separating when the cream is added. Mix in the lemon juice, then the cream, a little at a time, using a wooden spoon. Season to taste.

Brush 6 x 100ml (half-cup) dariole moulds with butter. Half fill each with mousse, add a scallop roe, then top up with more mousse. Tap each mould several times on a hard surface to settle the mousse and expel any air bubbles. Cover with a piece of buttered tinfoil.

Place the moulds in a tray and add water to halfway up the sides of the dariole moulds. Cook in a preheated 175°C (350°F) oven for 20–25 minutes. After 10 minutes place the rock lobster tails in the oven and bake them for the final 15 minutes.

SAUCES: Divide the shallots between 2 pots. Divide the fish stock, wine and vinegar between the same 2 pots.

To one pot add the saffron threads and to the other add the garlic and tomato paste. Reduce both down to approximately 100ml (half a cup) over a medium to high heat. Add half the cream to each reduction. Bring each to the boil, lower the heat. Simmer until each sauce just begins to thicken; 3–5 minutes.

Whisk a knob of butter into each and season them to taste. Pass both through a fine sieve into separate clean pots.

Remove the mousses and lobster tails from the heat and rest in a warm place for 5 minutes.

TO SERVE: Unwrap the rock lobster tails and slice them into 6 even portions. Run a small knife around the edge of each mousse and carefully turn each out onto a warm plate. Spoon on a little tomato sauce and place the rock lobster medallions on the top. Spoon the saffron sauce over the mousse.

Garnish with puff pastry fleurons and vegetable balls made with a small melon baller. Serve immediately.

NOTE: The rock lobster and the mousse must not be overcooked, and are therefore served warm, not piping hot. With this in mind, it is important that the plates and the sauces are well warmed.

SAUCES

2		shallots, finely diced
800ml	(3½ cups)	Fish Stock (see page 139)
250ml	(1 cup)	white wine
60ml	(4 tbsp)	champagne vinegar
1 pinch		saffron threads
½		clove garlic
1 tsp		tomato paste
500ml	(2¼ cups)	cream
2		knobs butter
		seasoning

PORT AND ORANGE GRANITE

Granite, or granita, as the Italians say, is the nearest thing there is to the original sorbet.

It is made using wine, tangy fruits, champagne and a little sugar. Due to the low sugar content small crystals form during the freezing process, thus a granite should always resemble crushed ice.

INGREDIENTS – SERVES 6-8

75g	(3 oz)	castor sugar
1 tbsp		water
		juice of 2 oranges
½		bottle good port

METHOD: Bring the sugar, water and orange juice slowly to the boil, and simmer for 1–2 minutes. Allow to cool completely, then pass into a clean bowl and add the port. Mix in well.

Pour into a flat, freezer-proof dish or tray and place in the freezer. When the liquid begins to freeze at the edges, give it a good stir. Repeat this process every so often according to how fine you want the crystals to be. Once completely frozen through, scrape the granite off the dish and spoon it into well-chilled glasses.

Serve immediately with fresh berries.

Today pheasants are bred on farms in New Zealand for release into the wild and for commercial resale. They are therefore available all year round, rather than just in the shooting season. Because of the farming, pheasant has all but been declassified as a game bird.

The farmed birds are generally of high quality and are graded according to size. They require very little or no ageing, although we prefer to leave them in the cooler for 3-4 days to develop the flavour. The best and most appropriate accompaniments for game birds are natural foods such as berries, chestnuts and watercress. Substitute pheasant meat from the thighs for the chicken in the savoury farce recipe.

BREAST OF PHEASANT

INGREDIENTS — SERVES 6

3	no. 2 size pheasants
approx 300g	Huka Lodge Savoury
(11 oz)	Farce (using the thigh meat; see page 136)
	ground pepper and salt
	clarified butter

SAUCE

700ml	(3 cups)	Brown Pheasant Stock (see page 140)
100ml	(½ cup)	port
1 dsp		redcurrant jelly
1 tsp		tomato paste
		sprig of thyme
200g	(7 oz)	blueberries
		knob unsalted butter
		seasoning

METHOD: Remove the breast from the pheasants by running a sharp knife around the contour of the rib cage. Cut the wing down to the first joint and clean the remaining bone free of all meat. Remove the thigh and drumstick from the main carcass. Slice through the joint between the drumstick and the thigh. Remove the bone and all skin and sinews from the thigh meat. Put the meat aside for the Savoury Farce (page 136).

Chop the carcass and use it for stock along with the wing and drumstick, as in Brown Pheasant Stock (recipe page 140).

SAUCE: Mix the stock, port, redcurrant jelly and tomato paste together in a heavy-bottomed pot, along with the sprig of thyme and a quarter of the blueberries. Reduce the liquid by two-thirds over a steady heat, pass into a clean pot and put aside until needed.

ASSEMBLING THE PHEASANT BREAST: Lay each pheasant breast on a flat surface, underside up. With a small sharp knife make an incision along the length of each breast, being careful not to cut right through. Carefully open out each side of the breast so a cavity is formed. Lightly season with pepper and salt and fill each cavity with savoury farce. Fold each side of the breast back in place, so it is back to its original shape, just slightly plumper. Turn over and lay on a flat tray.

Heat the clarified butter in a large, non-stick frypan until it is very hot. Quickly seal and brown each breast on both sides, underside first. Slowly roast in the oven at 175°C (350°F) for 8–10 minutes, or until just underdone. Remove from the heat and allow to rest in a warm place for 10 minutes before serving.

TO SERVE: Heat the sauce to serving temperature, whisk in a knob of butter and adjust the seasoning. Add the remaining blueberries.

Slice each pheasant breast into 3 pieces and place in the middle of each of 6 hot plates. Evenly pour over the blueberry sauce and garnish with fresh herbs. Servie with Dauphine Gratinée potatoes (see page 134) and mixed seasonal vegetables tossed in butter and thyme.

PEARS POACHED IN GRENADINE

Despite its appearance this dessert is not very difficult to make. Care must be taken in selecting the pears and not over- or undercooking them; if overcooked, they will not hold their shape.

The best pears to use are Williams, Winter Coles, or, if you can get them, Beurre Bosc pears. Whichever variety you choose buy them firm, with no blemishes or outer damage, then you will be able to cook them to the correct degree of softness.

The pears may be partially prepared a day ahead of serving. The quantities given for the liqueur creams are more than you will need, but I find this the minimum amount possible to enable easy construction of the dish. Any leftover cream is very nice to eat on its own and won't be wasted.

INGREDIENTS — SERVES 6

6		medium-sized firm pears
		enough water to just cover the pears
50ml	(3½ tbsp)	lemon juice
150g	(5 oz)	sugar
½		cinnamon stick
1		bayleaf
300ml	(1¼ cups)	grenadine

LIQUEUR CREAMS

200ml	(1 small cup)	milk
3		egg yolks
50g	(2 oz)	sugar
3		leaves gelatine or 10g (½ oz) powdered gelatine
200ml	(1 small cup)	cream
30ml	(2 tbsp)	cointreau
30ml	(2 tbsp)	raspberry liqueur

ORANGE CARAMEL SYRUP

100g	(4 oz)	castor sugar
240ml	(1 cup)	fresh orange juice
60ml	(4 tbsp)	crème de cacao (dark variety)
2g		arrowroot
		zest of 1 orange

METHOD: Add the lemon juice to the water. Peel and core the pears, leaving the stalk on, and hollow them out a little. Place in the lemon water.

Add the cinnamon, bayleaf and grenadine to the lemon water, and sprinkle over the sugar. Place over medium heat and bring to the boil. Lower the heat and simmer until the pears are still firm but beginning to cook through. Carefully remove the pears to a clean bowl then pour the liquid back over them. Allow the pears to completely cool in the liquid, thus ensuring the colour and flavours are absorbed. This can be done the day before, allowing the pears to completely chill in the refrigerator overnight.

Remove the pears from the liquid and place them on a clean towel, stalk end up, to drain off the excess. Leave in the refrigerator until ready for the next step.

LIQUEUR CREAMS: Bring the milk to the boil. Whisk the egg yolks and sugar together to the ribbon stage. Remove the milk from the heat and pour it onto the eggs, mixing as you go. Return to a gentle heat, stirring continuously with a wooden spoon until the mixture coats the back of the spoon. Do not boil. Remove from the heat.

Soak the gelatine leaves in water until soft, squeeze out and mix into the custard. Stir until completely dissolved, then pass through a fine sieve into a clean bowl. Allow to cool. Whip the cream and evenly mix it into the custard. Place one-third of the custard in a separate bowl. To the larger amount add the cointreau, and to the smaller amount add the raspberry liqueur. Allow to cool and thicken to the consistency of unbeaten egg yolk.

ASSEMBLING THE PEARS: Place the pears stalk down in a cup or dariole mould. Fill a small piping bag fitted with a small nozzle with raspberry liqueur cream. Using a small milk jug two-thirds fill each pear with cointreau cream, then immediately plunge the piping bag into the centre of the white cream and steadily squeeze until the cavity is filled. Quickly and carefully repeat with the remaining pears. Leave in the refrigerator until completely set.

ORANGE CARAMEL SYRUP: While the pears are setting, prepare the syrup. Place the sugar in a small, heavy-bottomed pot with 50ml (one-fifth) of the orange juice. Boil rapidly until the sugar caramelises to the colour of toffee. Cool slightly and carefully add the crème de cacao and the remaining juice.

Return to the heat to dissolve the caramel. Bring to the boil. Dilute the arrowroot and whisk it into the syrup.

Simmer for 1 minute. Pass through a fine sieve into a clean bowl. Add the zest. The heat in the syrup will extract the flavour and cook the zest. Cover and allow to completely cool out of the refrigerator. The consistency may be corrected with sugar syrup if necessary.

TO SERVE: Slice the pears in half to show the pattern inside, and arrange on cold plates. Spoon on the syrup and garnish with fresh fruit and mint. The pâte à décor cornets illustrated are optional.

SCALLOPS AND SALAD LEAVES WITH A WARM HERB VINAIGRETTE

In this recipe both the scallops and the vinaigrette should be just warm when served. We suggest you arrange the salad as you want to serve it, then at the last moment add the scallops and sprinkle over the vinaigrette. The combination of crisp salad greens and seafood is generally a very good one.

This dish can also be served as a luncheon dish; great in summer with a good Chardonnay or Sauvignon Blanc.

INGREDIENTS — SERVES 6

24	large scallops with pink roe
	clarified butter

SALAD

Use crisp heart leaves. The variety of salad leaves is optional, but these are our favourites.

12	butterhead lettuce leaves
6	curly or blanched endive leaves
12	red oak lettuce leaves
50g (2 oz)	julienne of carrot and leek, blanched
12	sprigs of chervil (fresh)

VINAIGRETTE

	juice of 1 lemon
½ tsp	whole grain mustard
½	clove garlic, crushed
1 tbsp	chopped mixed herbs (parsley, chervil, dill, chives)
2	shallots, sliced finely
10g (½ oz)	ginger root, finely diced and blanched
2 tbsp (3 tbsp)	white wine vinegar
125ml (½ cup)	salad oil
75ml (⅓ cup)	walnut oil
	salt and ground pepper

METHOD: Make the vinaigrette first and allow it to stand for 4 hours before serving. Mix together all the ingredients except the oil and seasoning, then pour on the oil, whisking as you go.

Season to taste with salt and ground pepper. Cover and allow to stand out of the refrigerator.

Trim the scallops, removing the tough muscles on the side. Cut the white meat in half, leaving the roe attached to one half. Put aside.

Arrange the salad leaves evenly on 6 plates. The plates should be at room temperature. Warm the vinaigrette through. Put aside but keep just warm.

Lightly season the scallops with salt and pepper. Heat a little clarified butter in a non-stick sauté or frypan. Sauté the scallop with the roe attached for 10 seconds each side, remove from the heat and keep warm. Sauté the remaining scallops the same way for 7 seconds each side. Place on kitchen paper on a tray and keep warm.

TO SERVE: Evenly divide the pieces of scallop between each salad, arranging them attractively over the leaves. Place a small bundle of carrot and leek julienne on the top. Sprinkle the vinaigrette over the salad and pour a little around it.

Garnish with fresh chervil and serve immediately.

The trick to this soup is to take good care in the preparation of the base stock, making sure all the ingredients are well cleaned and in good condition. Once the stock has come to the boil, make sure all the impurities are skimmed off, then turn it right down to a very gentle simmer. This way the stock will stay relatively clear.

ASPARAGUS ESSENCE

INGREDIENTS — SERVES 6

400g	(14 oz)	asparagus trimmings
1		medium-sized onion
50g	(2 oz)	celery
50g	(2 oz)	leek
25g	(1 oz)	butter
1		small bayleaf
6		white peppercorns
1		stalk parsley
3 litres	(5¼ cups)	Chicken Stock (see page 138)
		pepper and salt

GARNISH

10g	(½ oz)	carrot
10g	(½ oz)	red pepper
10g	(½ oz)	leek
10g	(½ oz)	asparagus
1 dsp		chopped chives or sprigs of chervil

METHOD: Clean and roughly chop all the vegetables for the soup. Melt the butter in a large pot, then lightly sweat the vegetables with the lid on, without allowing to colour. Add the bayleaf, peppercorns and parsley, then pour in the stock. Bring to the boil. Skim off all the impurities as they rise. Lower the heat and slowly simmer for 45 minutes to 1 hour.

During this time prepare the garnish. Peel the carrot, slice it thinly lengthways, then cut into thin strips approximately 5mm (1/6″) wide. Cut the strips into squares and blanch until tender in plenty of boiling salted water. Repeat this process with the red pepper and the leek. Thinly slice the asparagus into circles and quickly blanch. Refresh in iced water, drain, and put aside until needed.

Strain all the vegetables from the soup and put the stock into a clean pot. Over a gentle heat reduce the liquor to approximately 1500ml (2½ pints). Skim off any impurities as they rise to the surface.

TO SERVE: Heat the asparagus essence to serving temperature and season to taste with pepper and salt.

Mix the vegetable mosaics together and evenly divide them between 6 hot soup bowls. Pour over the soup then sprinkle with chopped chives or sprigs of chervil. Serve immediately.

FEIJOA AND LEMON SORBET WITH CHAMPAGNE

The feijoa is a native of Brazil, but is very common in New Zealand and Australia. The flavour is similar to that of pineapple and guava. Like most tropical and subtropical fruit, feijoas are ideal in sorbets. With the addition of fresh lemon juice the result is a bitter-sweet sorbet which is very refreshing.

METHOD: Add the sugar to the water and bring to the boil. Allow to cool completely. Purée the feijoa with the lemon juice then pass it through a fine sieve to remove the seeds etc. Add the purée to the sugar syrup and mix together.

Freeze immediately in a large stainless bowl, whisking from time to time to achieve a smooth and even texture. Alternatively, pour into a sorbetière or ice cream machine and freeze.

Serve in elegant glasses and at the last moment pour over the champagne. This is best done at the table.

Another serving suggestion is to scoop out the flesh of the feijoa, retaining the shells. Pipe the sorbet into the skin and serve as above.

INGREDIENTS — SERVES 6–8

350ml	(1½ cups)	water
90g	(3 oz)	sugar
400g	(14 oz)	ripe, peeled feijoa
		juice of 2 lemons
		your favourite champagne

This dish can be made with other cuts of pork such as loin, chops or even a roast. Whichever cut you choose, the meat must be a lovely pearl pink, fine in texture, and all visible fat must be milky white.

Take care to buy apples that are suitable for cooking, such as Granny Smith or Golden Delicious. Both these varieties will retain their shape when fried.

PORK FILLETS WITH FRIED APPLE

INGREDIENTS — SERVES 6

3		pork fillets (approx. 150g (5 oz) each after trimming)
18		quite thick apple wedges, free of skin and seeds
25g	(1 oz)	clarified butter
1 dsp		sugar

SAUCE

1		shallot, finely diced
50ml	(3½ tbsp)	cider vinegar
30ml	(2 tbsp)	calvados
700ml	(3 cups)	Brown Game Stock (see page 140)
		pepper and salt
		knob of butter

METHOD: Prepare the apples and store them in a little lemon water until needed. Place the diced shallot in a medium-sized pot with the vinegar and calvados. Reduce by half. Add the stock and reduce by two-thirds.

Meanwhile season each pork fillet with ground pepper and salt. Quickly brown on all sides over a high heat in a frypan. Place in a preheated 200°C (400°F) oven for 15–20 minutes or until just underdone. Remove from the heat, cover, and rest in a warm place for a further 10 minutes.

Heat the clarified butter in a large frypan. Thoroughly drain and dry the apple wedges and place them in the hot butter. Sprinkle with sugar and toss twice to evenly coat. Fry on both sides over medium heat until golden brown. The sugar will begin to caramelise. Remove from the heat and put aside, keeping warm until the next step.

TO SERVE: Heat the sauce to serving temperature. Pass into a clean pot and season to taste. Whisk in a knob of butter.

Evenly slice the pork into 6 portions and arrange on hot plates with 3 apple wedges each. Spoon over the sauce and garnish with fresh herbs. Serve immediately with roast potatoes, spinach and glazed carrots.

ALMOND WAFER BASKETS WITH FRESH FRUIT

INGREDIENTS — SERVES 6

WAFER

75g	(3 oz)	castor sugar
		pinch of cinnamon
1		egg
30g	(1 oz)	flour
1 tbsp		cream
5g		finely chopped almonds

FRUIT

1	punnet strawberries
1	punnet raspberries
½	punnet blueberries
24	pawpaw or melon balls
6	apple flans

COULIS

150g	(5 oz)	pawpaw
150g	(5 oz)	kiwifruit
150g	(5 oz)	raspberries
300ml	(1¼ cups)	Sugar Syrup (see page 146)

METHOD: Cream together the sugar, cinnamon and egg using a wooden spoon. Try not to froth the mixture or beat in air bubbles. Stir in the flour. Cover and rest in the refrigerator for 1 hour. Once the mixture is rested, mix in the cream. The consistency should be that of a batter.

Brush a baking sheet with plenty of butter then dust thoroughly with flour. With a 10cm (4″) plain cutter mark out 6 evenly spaced circles. Spread the batter evenly and thinly within each circle. Sprinkle on the finely chopped almonds.

Preheat the oven to 180°C (350°F).

Set out 6 brioche or similar moulds on the bench top ready to shape the wafers.

Great care must be taken at this stage. The wafers must be just set in the oven, with very little or no colour, and very floppy but not overly sticky. Bake for 2–3 minutes.

Now you must work quickly before the baking tray and the wafers cool. Slide a palette knife under each disc and lift it off the baking tray.

Drop into the mould and press into shape with your fingertips. If you find the last couple of wafers are too set and won't bend, return them to the oven for 30 seconds to heat up again, then press them into shape.

Once shaped, return the wafers to the oven and continue to bake until evenly browned; approximately 2 minutes.

Remove from the heat, allow to cool, then remove from the moulds. Store in an airtight container until required.

COULIS: Purée each fruit with 100ml (one-third) of the sugar syrup. Pass into a clean bowl. Correct the consistency and sweeten if need be. Refrigerate.

TO SERVE: Arrange the 3 coulis separately and evenly on 6 chilled plates. Place a wafer basket on each plate next to the coulis. Evenly divide the fruit and berries between the baskets. Dust with icing sugar and garnish with a sprig of mint.

FISH FUMET

This light but tasty soup can be made with several seafood combinations. John Dory and salmon are particularly well suited, as once cooked the flesh of both is quite firm and holds its shape. It is important once again to use a good quality base stock. Follow the instructions carefully in preparing Fish Stock (page 139) as its preparation will determine the success of the final soup. With a good stock in hand, this is very simple soup to make.

METHOD: Dice the fish into bite-sized pieces. Put aside until needed.

Bring the garlic, shallot and ginger to the boil in the white wine, and boil for 2 minutes. Add the carrot and boil a further minute. Add the fish stock and bring to the boil. Skim off any impurities as they rise. Now add the broccoli and leek. Simmer gently over a low heat for 4 minutes, continuing to skim off any impurities as the soup simmers.

TO SERVE: Bring the soup to serving temperature. Add the diced fish and diced tomato. Bring to the boil, adjust the seasoning, and skim. Serve immediately, garnished with the sliced spring onion.

INGREDIENTS — SERVES 6

500g	(1 lb)	cleaned John Dory
500g	(1 lb)	cleaned salmon
300ml	(1¼ cups)	dry white wine
1		clove garlic, crushed
2		shallots, finely diced
1 tsp		finely chopped ginger
1		medium-sized carrot, finely diced
1.2	litres (5 cups)	Fish Stock (see page 139)
12		small broccoli florets
3		baby leeks (white part only), sliced into rings
2		medium-sized tomatoes, skinned, seeded and diced salt and ground pepper
1		sliced spring onion

The tangy flavour of the apple, combined with the bite of the wine sauce, goes well with chicken in this recipe. I have designed it as an entrée but it could easily be adapted to serve as a main course.

SAUTÉED CHICKEN WITH APPLE

INGREDIENTS — SERVES 6

1		eating apple, Red Delicious or Cox
25g	(1 oz)	unsalted butter
6		small breasts of chicken, skin removed, trimmed clarified butter seasoning

SAUCE

500ml	(2¼ cups)	Chicken Stock (see page 138)
200ml	(1 cup)	Chablis
1		medium-sized shallot, finely diced
50ml	(3½ tbsp)	champagne vinegar or white wine vinegar
300ml	(1¼ cups)	cream
50g	(2 oz)	butter seasoning

METHOD: Mix the first 4 sauce ingredients together in a heavy-bottomed pot and reduce down to a syrupy consistency over medium heat. While the sauce is reducing, peel the apple and cut it into matchsticks. Lightly sweat the apple in the butter, being sure not to overcook it. Remove from the heat and reserve.

Add the cream to the reduction and slowly simmer until it is just beginning to thicken. Remove from the heat and reserve.

Heat the clarified butter in a frypan over a high heat. Season the chicken and sauté until brown on both sides.

Cook in a preheated oven at 175–190°C until just underdone. Remove from the heat and allow to rest for 5 minutes.

TO SERVE: Heat the sauce to serving temperature, and whisk in the butter a little at a time. Season and pass into a clean bowl.

Warm the apple and place a small bundle at the top of each warmed plate. Slice the chicken breasts across the breast and overlap onto the apple. Pour the sauce over evenly and garnish with sprigs of chervil. Serve at once.

RHUBARB GRANITE

Rhubarb has a very tart taste but makes delicious sorbets and granites. When buying fresh rhubarb look for stalks that are crisp and firm. Use them as soon as possible as they do not keep well. Remember a granite must give the impression of crushed ice.

INGREDIENTS — SERVES 6

400g	(14 oz)	fresh rhubarb
125g	(4 oz)	castor sugar
		juice of
		2 oranges
300ml	(1¼ cups)	water
		zest of ½ an
		orange, finely
		diced

METHOD: Cut the rhubarb into small pieces. Place all ingredients in a large pot and bring to the boil. Lower the heat and simmer until the rhubarb is very soft, approximately 15 minutes.

Allow to cool, then liquidise until very smooth. Pass the purée through a fine sieve and pour into a flat freezer-proof container. Freeze immediately.

As the liquid freezes, stir it regularly until it is completely frozen. The fineness of the granules will be determined by the number of times you stir the liquid during the freezing process.

TO SERVE: Scrape up the frozen liquid with a spoon and serve it in tall chilled glasses, garnished with fresh mint.

MARINATED SADDLE OF RABBIT

The saddles of rabbit must be put in the marinade the day before and left to marinate for 24 hours before cooking. We always use farmed rabbits which have been raised under strict regulations. Their quality is superb and the milky white flesh beautiful eating. The remainder of the carcass makes a lovely stock for the production of rabbit consommé and other soups.

INGREDIENTS — SERVES 6

3		saddles of rabbit, on the bone, from 1–1.5kg (2–3 lb) rabbits
50g	(2 oz)	clarified butter

MARINADE

60g	(2 oz)	small celery stick
1		small carrot, sliced
1		small onion, sliced
2 tbsp	(3 tbsp)	walnut oil
250ml	(1 cup)	red wine
200ml	(1 small cup)	port
2 tbsp	(3 tbsp)	white wine vinegar
300ml	(1¼ cups)	water
6		crushed peppercorns
1		clove garlic, crushed

SAUCE

400ml	(1¾ cups)	of the marinade
400ml	(1¾ cups)	Brown Game Stock (see page 140)
2 tsp		tomato paste
		salt and pepper
25g	(1 oz)	unsalted butter
3g	(1 heaped tsp)	arrowroot

ONION MARMALADE

2		medium-sized onions, thinly sliced
50ml	(3½ tbsp)	red wine vinegar
150ml	(⅔ cup)	red wine
		zest of ½ an orange
50g	(2 oz)	sultanas
		salt and pepper

METHOD: Remove the saddle from each rabbit and trim away the sinew etc. Put the meat aside until needed.

To prepare the marinade, quickly toss the vegetables in the walnut oil in a sauté pan. Do not allow to colour.

Place in a clean pot with all the remaining marinade ingredients. Bring to the boil and simmer gently for 20 minutes. Pass through a fine sieve into a clean container and allow to cool completely.

Place the whole rabbit saddles in the cold marinade 24 hours before intended use.

ONION MARMALADE: Place the sliced onion, vinegar, wine and zest in a heavy-bottomed pot. Place over a steady heat and reduce the liquid by half. Add the sultanas. Continue to reduce until most of the liquid has gone. Season to taste. The marmalade can also be made the day before and reheated in the microwave or in a covered pot over a gentle heat.

SAUCE: Drain the rabbit and put it aside until needed. Place 400ml (1¾ cups) of the marinade in a heavy-bottomed pot and add the game stock and tomato paste. Reduce by two-thirds over a steady heat. Dilute the arrowroot in a little red wine and mix into the sauce. Simmer 2 minutes. Pass through a fine sieve into a clean pot and season to taste. Put aside.

TO COOK AND SERVE: Carefully remove strips of meat from the bone. In a large frypan heat the clarified butter. Quickly brown the meat on all sides. Place in a preheated 200°C (400°F) oven for 5 minutes. Remove from the heat and rest in a warm place a further 5 minutes.

Rehead the onion marmalade and heat the sauce to serving temperature. Whisk in 25g (1 oz) of butter. Divide the onion between 6 hot plates. Thinly slice the rabbit and fan it over the onion. Spoon over the hot sauce and serve immediately with Fondant Potatoes (see page 134) and Spinach Subric (see page 130).

POACHED BABACO AND TAMARILLO

The tamarillo has quite an astringent taste but is good cooked and added to sweet sauces etc. The skin of the red tamarillo, which is inedible, should be a deep red when ripe. The fruit should be firm but give slightly when pressed.

The babaco, a large long fruit, is ready to eat when the skin has changed from green to yellow all over and is slightly aromatic. The babaco is a natural health food, high in vitamin C and papain, a digestive aid. It doesn't oxidise once cut and the pulp may be frozen. The babaco has no pips and the skin may also be eaten.

METHOD: Cut the babacos in half lengthways then cut into thick strips, cutting across the fruit. Poach in half the honey and sugar syrup until just tender. Allow to cool in the poaching liquid.

Plunge the tamarillos into boiling water then into iced water, and peel off the outer skin. In a clean pan poach the tamarillos in the remaining sugar syrup and honey. Allow to cool, then drain the fruit. Mix both poaching liquids together then pass into a clean bowl.

Place the egg yolks, castor sugar, grand marnier and orange juice in a sabayon basin and whisk over a bain marie until it has doubled in volume. Add the zest and continue to whisk to the ribbon stage.

TO SERVE: Cut the tamarillos into quarters lengthways and arrange 4 pieces on each serving plate. Arrange the babaco evenly around the tamarillo. Spoon some of the cool poaching liquid then the sabayon over the tamarillos. Serve immediately.

If desired, the dish may be flashed under a hot salamander or grill to brown the sabayon. The dish may also be served hot, by simply not allowing the fruit and syrup to cool.

INGREDIENTS — SERVES 6–8

2		average-sized babacos
6		red tamarillos
1 litre	(¾ pints)	Sugar Syrup (see page 146)
4 tbsp	(5 tbsp)	honey or treacle
5		egg yolks
100g	(4 oz)	castor sugar
60ml	(4 tbsp)	grand marnier juice of 1 orange zest of 1 orange, diced finely

Vichyssoise is traditionally served chilled, but in many restaurants it is also served hot. This soup may also be served chilled as a lunch soup on a hot summer's day, enjoyed with salads and a glass of dry white wine. Crème fraîche is a mixture of cream and buttermilk. Good quality crème fraîche is commercially available.

HOT WATERCRESS VICHYSSOISE

INGREDIENTS — SERVES 6

40g	(2 oz)	butter
75g	(3 oz)	onion, chopped
75g	(3 oz)	leeks, chopped
1		small clove garlic, crushed
1500ml	(2½ pints)	Chicken Stock (see page 138)
250ml	(1 cup)	white wine
400g	(14 oz)	potatoes, peeled and diced
1		small bunch watercress, plus 12 leaves for garnish seasoning
250ml	(1 cup)	cream
6 tbsps	(8 tbsps)	Crème Fraîche (see page 146) chopped chives

METHOD: Melt the butter in a heavy-bottomed pot. Add the onion, leek and garlic and sweat for a few minutes without colouring. Add the stock and wine, potato and watercress. Simmer for 35 minutes over a gentle heat, skimming off any impurities as they rise.

Remove from the heat and place in a liquidiser. Process until very smooth, then pass through a sieve into a clean pot. Bring back to the boil and season. Correct the consistency if necessary.

TO SERVE: Just before serving add the cream. Do not reboil. Divide between hot soup bowls, and spoon on the crème fraîche. Garnish with the watercress leaves, sprinkle with chopped chives and serve immediately.

POACHED
TAUPO TROUT

Over the years we have cooked trout many different ways, from very complicated to very simple dishes.

The following very simple method has proved the most successful. Trout is an earthy game fish; to over-prepare it will only spoil the fish and detract from that earthy character.

The condition of your trout is the most important factor. Big and long doesn't necessarily mean big on flavour, whereas a short fat fish with dark salmon-pink flesh will generally taste great. My personal preference is for rainbow trout over brown trout, but it's up to you!

METHOD: Roughly chop the bones, etc. Place them in a large pot and pour in the wine and water. Bring to the boil over a gentle heat, skimming off impurities as they rise. Add the remainder of the ingredients and simmer for 30 minutes. Pass through a fine sieve into a clean container. The stock may be used as is or reduced by half to concentrate the flavour. Allow to cool.

Season the fish with a little salt. Lightly butter a suitable poaching container and lay the fish in it. Just cover with stock. Poach over a gentle heat until the fish is just underdone, i.e. still a darker shade of pink inside.

Make a classic hollandaise sauce, adding 2 tablespoons of lemon juice.

TO SERVE: Place the trout on warmed plates, and coat in the lemon hollandaise. Garnish with julienne vegetables and sprigs of fennel, and serve immediately.

INGREDIENTS — SERVES 6

6 portions of trout, free from all bone and skin

STOCK

1kg	(2 lb)	trout bones and trimmings
500ml	(2¼ cups)	dry white wine
500ml	(2¼ cups)	water
1		bayleaf
25g	(1 oz)	chopped carrot
1		medium-sized onion, roughly chopped
25g	(1 oz)	chopped leek
1		stalk parsley
4		white peppercorns

CHAMPAGNE SPOOM

A spoom is the sweetest kind of sorbet and quite frothy. Meringue is folded into the prepared sorbet, then it is served in a tall, elegant glass. Spooms are usually made from sorbets using champagne or other wine.

INGREDIENTS
— SERVES 6–8

500ml	(2¼ cups)	Sugar Syrup (see page 146)
		juice of 2 lemons
300ml	(1¼ cups)	champagne or méthode champenoise wine
2		egg whites
100g	(4 oz)	castor sugar

METHOD: Mix the syrup, lemon juice and champagne together, then freeze in a sorbet machine or in the freezer, stirring regularly to ensure an even texture. Allow the sorbet to become a little firmer than usual.

Beat the egg whites to a stiff snow, adding the sugar slowly as you go.

Quickly mix the meringue into the sorbet just before serving. Serve immediately, as this type of sorbet will melt quite quickly.

LOIN OF LAMB AND PARSNIP MOUSSE

Lamb is basically a juicy, tender meat and must not be overcooked; it should remain pink and juicy inside.

When cooking smaller cuts of lamb such as loin, we achieve much better results by cooking the meat until it is just past rare, then removing it from the heat, covering it with a teatowel and resting it in a warm place for a further 10 minutes. The heat trapped inside will cook the meat to medium rare. The lamb will also 'relax' and allow all that fierce heat out, resulting in much more tender lamb. Ask your butcher to bone and trim the loin, leaving you a lean strip of meat. Retain the bones and trimmings to make the sauce.

The parsnip mousse is spread over an ovenproof container, baked, allowed to cool completely, then cut into shapes and sautéed to a golden brown in clarified butter. The flavours of parsnip and lamb combine wonderfully.

PARSNIP: Peel the parsnips, roughly chop them, and steam or boil in seasoned water until soft. Drain well and put into a heavy-bottomed pot with the cream. Reduce by half over a medium to high heat. Remove from the heat and allow to cool slightly.

Place in a liquidiser or food processor and process until very smooth, adding the egg as you go to aid the process. Make sure there are no lumps. Put into a clean bowl and season to taste.

Line a pie or flan dish with well-buttered greaseproof paper. Evenly spread the purée into the dish, approximately 5mm (¼″) thick. Bake in a preheated 170°C (340°F) oven for 15-20 minutes. Once set, remove the parsnip from the oven and allow it to cool completely, still in the dish. Once cool, turn it out of the dish onto a cutting board. Carefully peel off the paper and cut the parsnip into 12 small or 6 larger shapes: squares, diamonds or circles. Place on a clean dish and rest in the refrigerator until the next step.

SAUCE: Roughly chop all the vegetables and sauté them with the garlic in a little oil until well browned. Put aside.

Roast the bones and trimmings in a hot oven until dark brown, not burnt. Drain off all fat, and add the vegetables to the bones in the roasting tray. Add the redcurrant jelly and mix in. Add the port and simmer for 3 minutes over a high heat. Finally, add the water and herbs. Transfer the mixture into a clean pot and place over a gentle heat. Reduce by two-thirds, skimming off the impurities as they rise. Once reduced, pass the liquid through a fine sieve into a clean pot. Season to taste. If you desire, at this stage the jus may be very slightly thickened with arrowroot mixed with port. Be sure to simmer the jus for 3 minutes if doing so; you may have to pass it through the sieve again. Put the sauce aside until required, covering the surface with greaseproof paper to stop a skin from forming.

LAMB: Season the meat and sprinkle over a little chopped rosemary. Heat the clarified butter in a frypan over a high heat. Brown the meat on all sides, then place in a preheated 200°C (400°F) oven for 12–15 minutes, depending on how you like it done. Once done, remove the meat from the heat, and rest it in a warm place for a further 10 minutes.

Meanwhile sauté the parsnip mousse in clarified butter over a medium heat until golden on both sides. Keep it warm. Heat the sauce to serving temperature, and whisk in a knob of butter.

TO SERVE: Thinly slice the lamb into 6 even portions. Place the parsnip on hot plates and arrange the lamb evenly on each plate. Pour over the sauce. Garnish with fresh rosemary and serve immediately, accompanied by Ratatouille (see page 128) and Glazed Carrots (see page 131).

INGREDIENTS — SERVES 6

600g	(1¼ lb)	lean, trimmed lamb loin or strip loin seasoning
1 tsp		finely chopped rosemary clarified butter

SAUCE

1		medium-sized carrot
½		medium-sized onion
25g	(1 oz)	sliced leek oil
½		clove garlic, crushed all trimmings from the lamb and any bone, chopped (approx. 400g)
1 tbsp		redcurrant jelly
200ml	(1 small cup)	port
1 litre	(4½ cups)	cold water
½		bayleaf
1		sprig fresh rosemary seasoning knob of unsalted butter

SAUTÉED PARSNIP MOUSSE

300g	(10½ oz)	parsnip
300ml	(1¼ cups)	cream
2		eggs pepper and salt pinch nutmeg clarified butter

This is one of my favourite desserts, with its light, crumbly crust and melt-in-the-mouth filling. It is easy to prepare and cook. The sable or French shortbread pastry may be replaced by sweet or short sweet pastry, but sable is the best; it is the queen of all the sweet pastries.

PASSIONFRUIT AND LEMON TARTE

INGREDIENTS — SERVES 6

350g (12 oz)	Sable Pastry (see page 145)
6	ripe passionfruit
8	eggs
	juice of 1 lemon
200g (7 oz)	castor sugar
250ml (1 cup)	cream

SAUCE

	pulp from 6 passionfruit
100ml (½ cup)	Sugar Syrup (see page 146)

METHOD: Lightly flour a flat surface, and roll out the pastry to a thickness of aproximately 4mm (⅛″). Lightly butter a 22cm (9″) flan ring and place it on a buttered tray.

Carefully line the ring with sable. Do not overhandle or allow the pastry to become too warm or it will be impossible to work with. Line the pastry with a circle of greaseproof paper and blind bake by filling with beans or rice evenly over the surface. Rest in the refrigerator for 15 minutes, then bake in a preheated 175°C (350°F) oven for 8–10 minutes. Remove from the heat, remove the paper and beans or rice and allow the pastry to cool out of the refrigerator.

Cut the passionfruit in half and scoop out the pulp. Place the pulp in a liquidiser and process for a few seconds. Pass through a very fine sieve into a large bowl.

Break the eggs into the same bowl. Add the lemon juice and sugar, and whisk lightly until well mixed. Add the cream and mix in.

After checking there are no cracks in the pastry case, fill it with the egg and passionfruit mixture. Bake very slowly in a preheated 100°C (210°F) oven until the egg mixture is set; about 40–45 minutes. Once cooked, remove the tarte from the oven and allow it to cool slightly. Remove the flan ring and cool completely at room temperature.

SAUCE: Mix the passionfruit pulp and the sugar syrup together and place in a clean bowl.

TO SERVE: Slice the tarte into 6 pieces, dust with icing sugar, and place on serving plates. Spoon on a little sauce, garnish with a sprig of mint and enjoy!

AVOCADO
WITH PINE NUTS

This is a delightful dish. Light and refreshing, with contrasting tastes and textures, yet a wonderful marriage of flavours. Easy to prepare and inexpensive to produce, it's wonderful as a starter or combined with a salad as a summertime main dinner or luncheon course. Prepare all the accompanying ingredients first, then prepare the avocado just before serving.

METHOD: Purée the raspberries then pass them through a fine sieve into a clean bowl. Add all the other vinaigrette ingredients except the oil, salt and pepper, and mix together. Pour on the oil, mixing as you go. Season to taste with pepper and salt, then allow to stand at room temperature 1 hour before using.

Spread the pine nuts onto an oven tray and quickly roast under a hot grill until they begin to brown. Keep a close eye on them as they will brown quite rapidly. Allow to cool.

TO SERVE: Cut the avocados in half, remove the stones. Peel by pulling off the shell from the pointed end backwards. With a sharp knife, slice each half into a fan and position on a chilled plate. Sprinkle over the pine nuts then spoon over some vinaigrette. Garnish with fresh chervil and serve with salad leaves tossed in walnut oil.

INGREDIENTS — SERVES 6

3	ripe avocados (small to medium)
125g (4 oz)	pine nuts

VINAIGRETTE

50g (2 oz)	fresh or tinned raspberries
1	thinly sliced shallot
3 tbsp (4 tbsp)	white wine vinegar
	juice of 1 lemon
1 tsp	chopped chervil
½	clove garlic, crushed
	salt and ground pepper
100ml (½ cup)	olive oil
100ml (½ cup)	walnut oil

Fresh coriander, unlike the seeds, has quite a harsh flavour. Chopped and used sparingly, the flavour is superb, and its tang goes well with the sweetish flavour of carrot.

CARROT AND CORIANDER PURÉE

INGREDIENTS — SERVES 6

25g	(1 oz)	butter
50g	(2 oz)	chopped onion
50g	(2 oz)	chopped celery
50g	(2 oz)	chopped leek
500g	(1 lb)	sliced carrot
1 tsp		tomato paste
150ml	(⅔ cup)	dry white wine
1 litre	(4½ cups)	Chicken Stock (see page 138)
1 tsp		chopped coriander, plus 12 picked leaves
		salt and pepper
125ml	(½ cup)	cream

GARNISH

1		slice bread, for croûtons
60g	(2 oz)	clarified butter

METHOD: Melt the butter in a heavy-bottomed pot. Place all the washed and chopped vegetables in the pot and sweat them until tender. Add the tomato paste and cook for 1 minute over a medium heat. Add the wine. Do not colour the vegetables.

Add the stock and herbs and bring to the boil. Skim off all impurities as they rise. Lower the heat and gently simmer for 30–45 minutes.

Once done, remove from the heat and place in a liquidiser or food processor and blend until smooth. Push through a medium sieve into a clean pot. Adjust the seasoning.

GARNISH: Cut the slice of bread into small cubes. Heat the butter in a frypan and fry the cubes until they are golden all over, tossing regularly. Put aside until needed.

TO SERVE: Heat the soup to serving temperature. Add the cream and mix in; do not boil. Check the seasoning and consistency. Divide the soup between 6 hot soup bowls, sprinkle over a few croûtons and 2 coriander leaves to each bowl. Serve immediately.

LEMON AND WHISKY
SORBET

This would have to be my favourite sorbet, not surprisingly, as I not only enjoy sorbet but am rather partial to the occasional pure malt whisky.

INGREDIENTS — SERVES 6–8

450ml	(2 cups)	Sugar Syrup (see page 146)
		juice of 2 lemons
30ml	(2 tbsp)	whisky

METHOD: Mix all the ingredients together.

Place in the freezer and freeze to piping consistency, whisking vigorously at regular intervals to achieve a smooth texture. Alternatively, freeze in a sorbetière.

TO SERVE: Pipe into small glasses and garnish with a twist of lemon. Serve immediately.

BEEF DAUBE OVER
MIXED RICE

Daube is an ancient term for a type of meat stew with wine and spices, which has been braised in a closed earthenware casserole. The most popular is Boeuf en Daube à la Provençale, the recipe on which this one is based.

Traditionally there are stoned olives in the recipe, but we chose to omit them.

Canadian wild rice is actually the seed of an aquatic grass which is related to the rice family. It is expensive, but has a lovely nutty flavour and is well worth the expense. If wild rice is unavailable, brown rice is still very nice and is cheaper. It also has a nutty flavour. Both brown rice and wild rice take longer to cook than white polished rice. They must be cooked separately then mixed together once cooked.

INGREDIENTS — SERVES 6-8

900–1200g		
	(2–2½ lb)	topside of beef
100g	(4 oz)	streaky bacon
1		large onion
3		large cloves garlic
4 tbsp	(5 tbsp)	olive oil
		zest of ¼ of an orange
250ml	(1 cup)	red wine
60ml	(4 tbsp)	brandy
2		sprigs thyme
1		sprig parsley
1		bayleaf
1 tbsp		tomato paste
1 tbsp		red wine vinegar
55ml	(4 tbsp)	Beef Stock (see page 140)
		pinch mixed spice seasoning

RICE

125g	(4 oz)	Canadian wild rice or brown rice
100g	(4 oz)	long grain rice
200ml	(1 cup)	Chicken Stock (see page 138)
1		bayleaf
		knob of butter

GARNISH

6		bacon rashers, finely diced
		chopped parsley
6		sprigs fresh thyme

METHOD: Trim the meat then cut it into large pieces. Dice the bacon. Quarter then slice the onion, crush the garlic.

Heat the olive oil in a large frypan then fry the bacon, onion and garlic until they begin to brown, 5–10 minutes. Once fried, transfer onto a clean plate and put aside.

Place the cubed meat in a suitable dish, and mix in the onion, garlic, bacon and orange zest.

Pour over the red wine, brandy and herbs. Leave to marinate for 4–5 hours, mixing occasionally.

Heat the same frypan, adding more oil if necessary. Drain the marinated meat, retaining the marinade. Brown the meat on all sides in batches, then transfer it to an ovenproof casserole. Mix in the tomato paste, marinade, vinegar, beef stock, mixed spice and ground pepper. Be careful when seasoning as the bacon will possibly make the daube salty enough.

Preheat the oven to 150° C (300° F). Cover the casserole and slowly cook 1½–2 hours.

WILD RICE: Bring to the boil in plenty of salted water, drain, just cover in more salted water then simmer until tender; approximately 15–20 minutes.

Cook brown rice the same way but it will take slightly less time to become tender.

LONG GRAIN RICE: Rinse under cold running water if necessary.

Cover the long grain rice with the stock, season with a little salt, and add the bayleaf. Bring to the boil. Lower the heat to a gentle simmer and cover the pot with a lid. Cook for 15–20 minutes. Remove from the heat, mix in a knob of butter and add the brown or wild rice and mix together. Remove the bayleaf.

GARNISH: Mix together the bacon and parsley then roll into even balls, about 3 per portion. Quickly sauté in hot oil then put aside for garnish.

TO SERVE: Remove the daube from the oven and check the consistency and seasoning. Remove the bayleaf. Divide the rice between 6 hot plates and make a nest. Spoon in the beef daube. Sprinkle over the bacon balls.

Sprinkle around crisp Baby Vegetables (see page 130) blanched and tossed in Beurre Fondue (see page 132). Garnish with fresh thyme and serve.

CINNAMON ICED SOUFFLÉ

This is a light aerated type of ice cream or iced parfait which is easy and quick to prepare. Make it the day before you intend to serve it, thus allowing time for it to freeze evenly.

Freeze individual soufflés in ramekins with the sides built up with tinfoil.

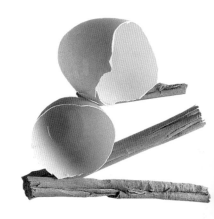

ICED SOUFFLÉ: Whisk the yolks, sugar and cinnamon to the ribbon stage in a large bowl over a bain marie. Ensure all the sugar dissolves. Allow to cool, whisking regularly.

Whisk the cream until the whisk leaves tracks. Whisk the egg whites until fluffy.

Fold the cream into the sabayon, ensuring it is evenly mixed in. Carefully fold in the egg whites. Do not overmix, or tap the container, or you will knock the air out. Pour into prepared ramekins or other suitable containers and freeze.

SAUCE: Place the yolks, sugar and rum in a bowl. Whisk together well, until the mixture doubles in volume. Add the coffee to the milk and place over a medium heat in a heavy-bottomed pot. Bring to the boil. Pour the hot milk onto the egg mixture, stirring as you go. Return to a clean pot and place over a gentle heat, stirring continuously with a wooden spoon. On no account allow the custard to boil. Cook until it forms a coating consistency, then pass through a fine sieve into a clean bowl. Allow to cool completely, stirring from time to time. Cover to prevent a skin from forming.

TO SERVE: Unmould the iced soufflé by dipping the container briefly in warm water and tipping it upside down onto a cutting surface. Evenly slice with a hot knife onto 6 chilled plates, spoon on a little coffee sauce and garnish with fresh berries and chocolate leaves. Serve immediately.

NOTE: If serving more than 1 or 2 portions, we suggest you have all your plates set up ready, requiring only the positioning of the iced soufflé itself . . . otherwise you may find you are serving a milkshake!

INGREDIENTS — SERVES 6–8

SOUFFLÉ

5		egg yolks
110g	(4 oz)	castor sugar
2 tsp		cinnamon powder
300ml	(1¼ cups)	cream
2		egg whites

COFFEE CREAM SAUCE

6		egg yolks
100g	(4 oz)	castor sugar
30ml	(2 tbsp)	rum (optional)
450ml	(¾ pint)	milk
1 tsp		granulated instant coffee

FRESH TAUPO TROUT SASHIMI STYLE

Recently we were told by a party of Japanese guests at the Lodge that trout wasn't one of the fish usually served as sashimi. That was before they had tried sashimi prepared with some of the trout they had just caught. Even they were impressed by the delicate flavour and texture of the fish.

If serving trout this way, make certain the fish you use is very fresh and in excellent condition, with deep salmon-pink flesh. All the accompanying authentic Japanese products are readily available in New Zealand.

The quantities depend on how much you intend to eat and how big your fish is. The soy sauce and wasabi are just for dipping so you do not need large quantities.

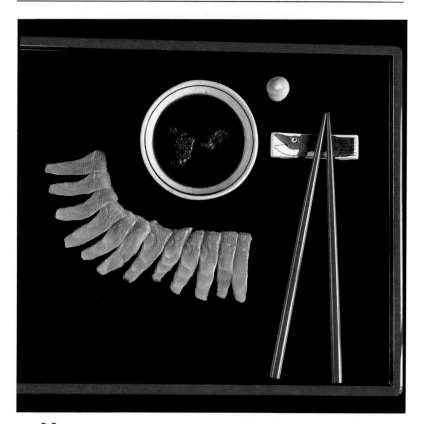

INGREDIENTS

fresh trout, approx. 60g (2 oz) per portion
good quality Japanese soy sauce
Japanese wasabi mustard
a little salt
dill or fennel to garnish

METHOD: Fillet the trout, making sure all the skin and bones are removed. Trim off some of the brown flesh found just under the skin.

Cut the fillets into 4cm (1½″) wide strips, then with a very sharp knife slice the strips into very thin slithers, cutting across the fish. Arrange the fish attractively on a plate around a small dish of soy sauce. Garnish with the fennel or dill and sprinkle with a little salt. On a separate dish serve some green wasabi mustard. If you like, serve a small salad on a side plate.

WHITE ONION SOUP
WITH CIDER AND APPLE

The tang of the cider and the bite of the apple combine superbly with the velvety texture of the onion soup.

This is one of the few soups we make using flour. Therefore it is a slightly heavier soup, more suited to a cold winter's evening.

METHOD: Gently cook all the sliced vegetables in the butter with the lid on until tender. Do not allow to colour. Add the flour and cook for a few minutes over a gentle heat.

Add the cold stock, cider and cider vinegar and mix well. Add the bayleaf. Bring to the boil, stirring regularly, and skimming off any impurities. Lower the heat and gently simmer for 30 minutes, skimming when necessary. Remove the bayleaf.

Pass through a medium sieve into a clean pot, as many of the vegetables as possible. Season to taste and put aside until required.

GARNISH: Cut the bread into small cubes and fry in clarified butter until golden all over. Toss regularly to ensure even colouring. Place on kitchen paper to drain off the excess butter.

Cut the apple into matchsticks and quickly blanch in lemon water. Cool.

Sauté the onion without allowing to colour, then drain well on kitchen paper.

TO SERVE: Heat the soup to serving temperature, add the cream. Divide the sautéed onion between 6 hot soup bowls. Pour on the hot soup. Sprinkle over a few apple matchsticks and croûtons, then place a sprig of chervil on top. Serve immediately.

INGREDIENTS — SERVES 6

50g	(2 oz)	unsalted butter
100g	(4 oz)	onions, thinly sliced
50g	(2 oz)	sliced leek
50g	(2 oz)	sliced celery
50g	(2 oz)	flour
1350ml	(2¼ pints)	Chicken Stock (see page 138)
100ml	(½ cup)	dry cider
50ml	(3½ tbsp)	cider vinegar
1		small bayleaf
		salt and ground pepper
50ml	(3½ tbsp)	cream

GARNISH

1		slice of bread, for croûtons
100g	(4 oz)	apple
200g	(7 oz)	thinly sliced onion sautéed in a little butter
6		sprigs fresh chervil

PAWPAW AND PORT SORBET

Pawpaw, like most tropical fruit, is perfectly suited to sorbets. The smooth, perfumed character is most refreshing and a delightful result is always achieved. With the addition of the port, another dimension is reached, giving body and depth.

INGREDIENTS — SERVES 6

350ml	(1½ cups)	water
90g	(3 oz)	castor sugar
400g	(14 oz)	ripe, peeled pawpaw
about	45ml (3 tbsp)	port
		juice of 1 lemon

METHOD: Boil the water and sugar together. Simmer for 3 minutes over a gentle heat. Allow to cool completely.

Purée the pawpaw with the port in a food processor. Add the lemon juice. Pass through a fine sieve into a clean bowl, pushing through as much of the pulp as possible.

When the syrup is cool, mix it with the purée. Freeze immediately in a sorbetière or in the freezer, whisking regularly to achieve an even texture.

Serve in chilled glasses, topped by small dice of pawpaw.

RACK OF LAMB

Three of our favourites: nice pink lamb, fresh crisp salad leaves and gratined dauphine potatoes lightly flavoured with garlic; all combined with the bitter-sweet flavour of the oranges.

LAMB: Brush the best-ends with oil and liberally sprinkle with black pepper and herbs.

Brown lightly on the stove top, then roast in the oven for 10–15 minutes at 200°C (400°F). When done, remove from the oven and rest in a warm place for a further 20 minutes.

CARAMELISED ORANGES: Preheat the oven grill to very hot. Dissolve the brown sugar in the butter then brush it over the orange segments. Caramelise under the grill for 20 seconds. Do not cook through or the orange will fall to pieces. Keep in a warm place.

SALAD: Wash the lettuce leaves, then pour the oil and salt into a clean bowl, and toss the leaves in the oil.

TO SERVE: Arrange the salad evenly on 6 warm plates. Carefully slice the best-ends into cutlets, place 3 on each plate, then place 2 orange segments on each.

Serve with a vinaigrette. This is a warm dish; too hot or too cold will spoil the flavours. Ideal for a light luncheon or dinner. Serve with Dauphine Potatoes (see page 134).

INGREDIENTS — SERVES 6

LAMB

3	whole best-ends, 6 cutlets each, trimmed and skinned
	hazelnut or walnut oil
	ground black pepper
	salt
2 tbsp	mixed herbs

CARAMELISED ORANGES

36	orange segments, free of pith
8 dsp	brown sugar
4 tbsp (5 tbsp)	clarified butter

SALAD

Use any salad combination you like; our favourites are as follows.

24	leaves lambs' lettuce
12	red oak lettuce leaves
6	leaves butterhead lettuce
3 tbsp (4 tbsp)	hazelnut oil
	pinch of salt

RHUBARB MOUSSE

For this dessert be sure to buy fresh, crisp rhubarb with plenty of colour, so the resulting mousse is a lovely pastel red colour. Combined with the fresh berries, this is a light, refreshing dessert, abundant with bitter-sweet, fruity flavours.

INGREDIENTS — SERVES 6

400g (14 oz)	fresh rhubarb
900ml (3¾ cups)	water
250g (9 oz)	sugar
	juice of 1 lime
	juice of 1 lemon
	juice of 1 orange
3	leaves gelatine or
	1 tbsp powdered
	gelatine
200ml (1 cup)	cream
1	egg white

BERRIES

Use any combination of berries. This combination is particularly delicious.

6	medium-sized strawberries, cut into quarters
30	raspberries
24	blueberries
18	blackberries
6	sprigs mint

SYRUP

approx. 400ml (1¾ cups) reduced poaching liquid (see method)
1–2g (½–1 tsp) arrowroot

METHOD: Wash rhubarb and cut it into 2.5cm (1″) lengths. Place in a medium-sized heavy-bottomed pot. Add the water, sugar and all the fruit juice. Place over medium to high heat and cook until the rhubarb is quite soft.

Remove the rhubarb from the cooking liquid with a slotted spoon or sieve. Place in the food processor and process until very smooth. While still hot, place in a clean bowl.

Soak the gelatine leaves in cold water, or dissolve powdered gelatine in a little cold water, then add to the hot rhubarb purée. Stir continuously until all the gelatine is dissolved. If necessary, return to a gentle heat and stir until dissolved.

Push the purée through a fine sieve into a clean bowl. Cool over ice, stirring from time to time to ensure even cooling.

SYRUP: Return the poaching liquid to a high heat and reduce by two-thirds, to approximately 400ml (1¾ cups). Skim off any impurities as they rise during the reduction.

Dilute the arrowroot in a little water and whisk into the liquid. Simmer for 3 minutes. Pass through a fine sieve into a clean bowl, cover and allow to cool completely. Put aside until needed.

MOUSSE: Lightly whip the cream and beat the egg white to a soft, fluffy consistency.

Allow the purée to set to the consistency of unbeaten egg white, then evenly mix in the whipped cream. Finally, fold in the whisked egg white carefully — don't overmix at this stage or the light and airy effect will be lost.

Evenly divide the mousse between 6 small moulds and place them in the refrigerator for at least one and a half hours.

TO SERVE: Unmould the mousses onto chilled plates by quickly dipping the containers into warm water then shaking them out.

Sprinkle the prepared and washed berries around the rhubarb mousse. Spoon cool syrup over the fruit and around the mousse. Garnish with a sprig of fresh mint.

BUTTON MUSHROOM TERRINE

M E N U

10

This terrine is a variation of our original recipe, made with a variety of exotic, imported wild mushrooms, such as cèpes, morels and chanterelles. These are all beautiful mushrooms but are very expensive and can be difficult to come by. With this in mind, we have developed the dish using only button mushrooms, which are easily available and not too expensive. The mushrooms should be evenly sized and firm.

The resulting terrine combines beautifully with the vinaigrette, and looks very handsome.

It is possible to make individual mushroom terrines, but much less trouble to use a 1.2-litre terrine mould.

METHOD: Place the lemon juice in a flat pot or pan, add the washed mushrooms, and toss them in the juice, making sure they are all coated. Add enough water to almost cover the mushrooms. Season with salt and pepper. Place over a high heat and cook until just firm. Drain and pat dry with kitchen paper.

Warm the consommé and add the gelatine. Stir slowly over a gentle heat until completely dissolved. Season to taste with pepper and salt. Pass through a fine sieve into a clean bowl and set aside until cool.

CONSTRUCTION: Chill the terrine mould. Cover the bottom of the mould with cool jelly, about 5mm (¼") deep. Sprinkle over half the chopped herbs. Allow to set.

Evenly lay about a third of the mushrooms the length of the terrine. Just cover with another layer of jelly, and allow to set. Sprinkle over the remaining herbs and repeat the above process until there are 3 layers of mushrooms set in aspic. Cover and place in the refrigerator for 3 hours before serving.

TO SERVE: Slice the terrine onto serving plates. Leave for 20–25 minutes to reach room temperature, to increase the flavours. Spoon the vinaigrette (also at room temperature) around each slice and serve.

INGREDIENTS –
SERVES ABOUT 15

TERRINE

30ml	(2 tbsp)	lemon juice
about	90	small to medium button mushrooms ground pepper and salt
700ml	(3 cups)	poultry Consommé (see page 22)
	7	leaves gelatine, soaked in cold water and squeezed dry, or 3 ½ tbsp (5 tbsp) gelatine powder
2 tbsp	(3 tbsp)	chopped chives
2 tbsp	(3 tbsp)	chopped parsley
2 tbsp	(3 tbsp)	chopped chervil

HUKA LODGE VINAIGRETTE

(see page 136)

Although frozen mussels are suitable for the preparation of chowder, we prefer fresh. When buying live mussels, choose the small or medium-sized ones, which are better eating, even in soups. Check that the shells are firmly closed and undamaged, and that the fish is still moist. Discard any that float before they are cooked, as these are dead, and scrub the outside of the shells to remove any grit etc. before cooking.

If desired, the yoghurt may be replaced by crème fraîche or regular cream, although we find that natural yoghurt gives the chowder an interesting 'bite'.

MUSSEL CHOWDER

INGREDIENTS — SERVES 6

approx.

1.4 kg	(3 lb)	mussels (to give 400g (1 lb) meat when shells removed)
200ml	(1 cup)	dry white wine
50g	(2 oz)	finely diced onion
50g	(2 oz)	finely diced leek
50g	(2 oz)	finely diced carrot
50g	(2 oz)	finely diced celery
1		small clove garlic, crushed
1		bayleaf
200g	(7 oz)	diced potato
1200ml	(2 pints)	Fish Stock (see page 139)
2 tbsp	(3 tbsp)	chopped parsley
3		medium-sized tomatoes, skinned, seeded and diced

CHERVIL YOGHURT

		juice of 1 lemon
100ml	(½ cup)	unsweetened plain yoghurt
2 tbsp	(3 tbsp)	chopped chervil ground pepper and salt

METHOD: Clean the mussels and place them in a large pot with a little white wine. Cook over a high heat until the mussels open. Remove from the liquid and allow to cool. Remove the mussels from the shell and trim off the hard white tendon. Finely mince the mussels.

Cook the diced vegetables and garlic in white wine without allowing to colour. Add the bayleaf and potato. Pour on the stock and simmer for 8 minutes, skimming when necessary. Add the mussels and simmer for a further 6 minutes, again skimming when necessary. Remove the bayleaf. Add the chopped parsley and diced tomato. Season to taste.

YOGHURT: Mix the lemon juice with the yoghurt, add the chervil, and season with a little pepper and salt.

TO SERVE: Heat the chowder to serving temperature and divide between 6 hot soup bowls. Spoon on a swirl of chervil yoghurt and serve.

NOTE: If desired, 100ml (½ cup) cream may be added to the chowder just before serving.

BLUEBERRY SPOOM

Fresh blueberries are best in this recipe, but out of season we often use bottled berries and find a very good result is obtained.

METHOD: Mix the syrup and lemon juice together. Place the blueberries in the liquidiser and process until smooth. Pass into a clean bowl then mix in the sugar syrup and juice. Freeze until firmer than a normal sorbet, whisking from time to time to achieve a smooth texture. Alternatively, process in a sorbetière.

Beat the egg whites to a stiff snow, adding the sugar slowly as you go.

Quickly mix the meringue into the sorbet just before serving. This sorbet will melt quickly. Garnish with fresh blueberries and serve in chilled glasses.

INGREDIENTS — SERVES 6–8

500ml	(2¼ cups)	Sugar Syrup (see page 146)
		juice of 1 lemon
300g	(11 oz)	blueberries
2		egg whites
100g	(4 oz)	castor sugar

We prefer to use fillet steak or tenderloin in this dish as tenderness and flavour are guaranteed. Nevertheless, other prime beef cuts, such as sirloin or rump, are also suitable. Whatever cut you use, remember to rest the beef for 10 minutes after cooking to prevent the loss of natural juices.

PRIME BEEF IN A SHALLOT AND MARSALA GLAZE

INGREDIENTS — SERVES 6

6		prime beef steaks, between 100–150g (4–5oz) each
2 tbsp	(3 tbsp)	walnut oil
		ground pepper and salt

SAUCE

100ml	(½ cup)	red wine
700ml	(3 cups)	Brown Veal Stock (see page 140)
3		shallots, finely sliced
10g	(½ oz)	clarified butter
30ml	(2 tbsp)	marsala
40g	(1½ oz)	unsalted butter
		ground pepper and salt

METHOD: Heat the walnut oil in a frypan over a high heat. Season the meat and brown it on all sides, sealing all the outer surfaces. Put aside.

Pour the excess oil out of the frypan and return the pan to a medium heat. Add the red wine to the pan, thus taking advantage of the flavours in the sediment left from sealing the beef. Simmer the red wine for 1 minute then strain it through a fine sieve into a heavy-bottomed pot. Add the brown stock and reduce by two-thirds over a steady heat.

In a small pot sweat the shallots in the clarified butter; do not allow to colour. Strain the reduced stock and red wine onto the shallots, bring to the boil and skim off any impurities. Add the marsala, season to taste. Put aside until required.

TO SERVE: Cook the beef to the desired degree in a preheated 200°C (400°F) oven; rare is best. Heat the sauce to serving temperature then whisk in the unsalted butter a nob at a time. Try not to boil the sauce once the butter has been added. Slice each steak into 3 pieces and fan onto a hot plate.

Evenly pour over the shallot and marsala sauce. Garnish with fresh herbs and serve with Roast Châteaux Potatoes (page 134) and crisp seasonal vegetables.

GRAND MARNIER YOGHURT CREAM

YOGHURT CREAM: Soak the gelatine leaves in water until soft. Squeeze dry. Warm the orange juice and the grand marnier, add the sugar and dissolve. Add the gelatine powder or softened leaves and stir over a very gentle heat until completely dissolved. Cool, then stir in the yoghurt. Pass into a clean bowl and allow to cool. Half whip the cream and beat the egg white until fluffy. Fold the cream into the yoghurt, then very carefully fold in the egg white. Fill 6–8 small jelly or dariole moulds with the yoghurt cream mixture and allow to set in the refrigerator for at least 1 hour.

TUILES: Place all the ingredients except the orange zest in a bowl or food processor and mix until very smooth. Mix in the zest.

Liberally brush a baking tray with butter then dust with flour. Tap off excess flour. Cook the tuiles in batches of 4–6. Mark out 10cm (4″) circles then thinly spread the batter to the marked size. Cook in a preheated oven at 190°C (375°F) for 3–5 minutes, until dark brown round the edges and golden in the centre. Remove from the oven and, while still hot, use a flexible palette knife to remove the tuiles from the tray. Place them over a rolling pin and allow to cool completely.

When cool, carefully remove the tuiles and store them in an airtight container until needed.

TO SERVE: Turn out the yoghurt creams onto a chilled plate and garnish with orange segments.

Warm the orange juice for the sabayon and dissolve the sugar in it. Whisk the egg yolks in a sabayon basin or round bowl until fluffy and pale in colour. Pour on the orange juice and sugar, whisking as you go. Place over a gentle heat and continue to whisk until the whisk leaves tracks. Spoon half the sabayon on and the rest around the yoghurt creams. Serve 2 orange tuiles with each and garnish with a sprig of fresh mint.

Yoghurt desserts are by no means a new thing; they have been enjoyed for many centuries in some tropical regions. Indian cuisine has always incorporated a wide variety of yoghurt desserts.

Yoghurt and fruits have deliciously complemented each other in many a modern menu, and the addition of fruit-flavoured or fruit-based liqueurs is another easy variation, again resulting in some delicious desserts.

The crispness of the featherlight tuiles makes a delightful texture variation with this smooth dessert.

INGREDIENTS — SERVES 6–8

YOGHURT CREAM

3		leaves gelatine or 1 tbsp powered gelatine
		juice of 1 orange
60ml	(4 tbsp)	grand marnier
50g	(2 oz)	castor sugar
175ml	(¾ cup)	plain unsweetened yoghurt
150ml	(⅔ cup)	cream
1		egg white
		orange segments, for garnish

SABAYON

		juice of 3 oranges
100g	(4 oz)	castor sugar
6		egg yolks

TUILES

60g		unsalted butter
2		egg whites
110g	(4 oz)	castor sugar
		pinch salt
60g	(2 oz)	flour
2 dsp		very finely diced orange zest
		butter and flour for baking tray

MARINATED TAUPO TROUT

This dish should be prepared 24 hours before serving.

The most important factor in its production is that the trout must be very fresh and in perfect condition, with deep salmon-pink flesh. As the trout is eaten virtually raw this is essential. Serve with a salad, hard-boiled egg and finely chopped onion.

METHOD: Fillet the fish and remove all bones, leaving the skin on. Make 4 small incisions on the skin side, just cutting through the skin. Sprinkle salt over the fish and work it in just a little. Sprinkle over the chopped dill and lightly pat down. Mix the sugar, lemon and oil together.

Place the fillet on a tray and leave for 4 hours, then pour over the oil mixture. Leave in a cool place to marinate, basting with oil every so often. The next day, remove the fish from the liquid and pat it dry.

TO SERVE: Place rows of prepared garnish on one side of a plate. Very thinly slice the trout and lay it on the plate. Garnish with a sprig of dill. Serve immediately with a salad and brown bread.

INGREDIENTS — SERVES 6–8

1 x 500–800g		
	(1–1¾ lb)	side fresh trout
30g	(1 oz)	salt
50g	(2 oz)	fresh chopped dill
50g	(2 oz)	brown sugar
		juice of 2 lemons
100ml	(½ cup)	olive oil

GARNISH

		salad leaves of your choice
2 tbsp	(3 tbsp)	sieved, hard-boiled egg white
2 tbsp	(3 tbsp)	sieved, hard-boiled egg yolk
1 tbsp		finely chopped parsley
2 tbsp	(3 tbsp)	finely chopped onion

CHICKEN AND BLUE CHEESE POTAGE WITH BUTTON MUSHROOMS

Originally we thickened this soup by making a roux, but we now use vegetable bulk to thicken it, thus eliminating the need for any flour. The process is similar to most vegetable purées, and is very simple.

METHOD: Wash and clean all the vegetables; roughly chop the onion, celery and leek. Melt the butter in a large pot over a medium heat. Add the vegetables, except the potato, then add the blue cheese. Cook with the lid on for 3–5 minutes, without allowing to colour, stirring occasionally. Add the wine and continue to cook for 2 minutes. Remove the lid. Add all the stock and the bayleaf. Add the potato, washed, peeled and roughly chopped. Bring to the boil, skim, then simmer for 20–30 minutes. Skim when needed.

Once cooked, remove the soup from the heat, place it in a liquidiser or food processor, and process until very smooth. Strain through a medium sieve into a clean pot, pushing as much of the vegetable purée through the sieve as possible. Season to taste. Put aside.

GARNISH: Finely dice the pre-cooked chicken. Wash the mushrooms, then slice and lightly cook them in lemon juice and water. Remove from the heat and drain.

TO SERVE: Heat the soup to serving temperature, and add the cream. Do not reboil.

Divide the diced chicken and blue cheese pieces between 6 hot soup bowls. Pour on the soup. Evenly sprinkle over the sliced mushrooms and finely chopped chives. Serve while hot.

INGREDIENTS — SERVES 6

100g (4 oz)	onion
100g (4 oz)	celery
50g (2 oz)	leek
300g (11 oz)	potato
25g (1 oz)	unsalted butter
100g (4 oz)	blue vein cheese, broken into small pieces
200ml (1 cup)	dry white wine
1200ml (5 cups)	Chicken Stock (see page 138)
1	bayleaf
	seasoning
50ml (3½ tbsp)	cream

GARNISH

60g (2 oz)	diced cooked chicken
24	small button mushrooms, sliced
	juice of 1 lemon
	a little water
	small pieces of blue cheese
1 dsp	finely chopped chives

TROPICAL FRUIT SORBET

INGREDIENTS — SERVES 6–8

250ml	(1 cup)	water
80g	(3 oz)	sugar
200g	(7 oz)	pawpaw, peeled, seeds removed
200g	(7 oz)	mango, peeled juice of 1 grapefruit

Any combination of tropical fruits will make a nice sorbet, but there is something about pawpaw and mango which makes this combination hard to beat.

METHOD: Add the sugar to the water and bring to the boil. Simmer for 3 minutes, then allow to cool completely. Add the grapefruit juice to the peeled pawpaw and mango, and purée until very smooth. Combine with the cold sugar syrup and purée together.

Pass through a fine sieve into a suitable container. Freeze in a sorbetière or place in a stainless steel bowl in the freezer, whisking regularly to achieve a smooth finish. Serve immediately.

LAMB MEDALLIONS

Ask your butcher for boned strip loin of lamb, but retain the bones for the sauce. There are commercial sauces and sauce flavourings on the market but making your own is much more satisfying.

NOODLES: Remove the seeds from the pimento, roughly chop, then liquidise with the egg whites. Push through a fine sieve into the egg yolks. Proceed as in the Basic Noodle Dough recipe (page 137), making tagliatelle-type noodles. Cook, drain and put aside until required. Leave a little water or oil in the noodles so they don't stick together.

SAUCE: Brown the bones and vegetables well in a hot oven. Once done, place in a clean pot and cover with cold water (at least 1 litre). Add the rosemary and garlic. Place over a high heat and bring to the boil. Skim, then reduce the heat and gently simmer for half to three-quarters of an hour. Pass the stock through a sieve into a clean pot and reduce over a high heat by three-quarters, until a highly flavoured, dark brown essence is achieved.

Add the cream then slowly simmer for 5 minutes. Put aside until required.

THE LAMB: Season the lamb with ground pepper and salt. Brown quickly in hot oil on the stove top, then cook with the whole cloves of garlic in a preheated 200° C (400° F) oven for 10–15 minutes.

Remove from the heat and rest for a further 10 minutes. Retain the roasted garlic cloves.

TO SERVE: Reheat the sauce to serving temperature, then whisk in the butter a little at a time. Season to taste.

Reheat the noodles in a covered tray in the oven or the microwave, then carefully toss in the sauce. Slice the roasted garlic cloves very thinly. Evenly divide the noodles between 6 hot plates and sprinkle over the sliced garlic.

Thinly slice the lamb into 6 even portions and arrange them over the noodles. Garnish with a sprig of rosemary and chopped spring onion.

Serve immediately with crisp baby carrots, courgettes and broccoli florets.

INGREDIENTS — SERVES 6

500g	(1 lb)	lamb strip loin, trimmed and boned (approx. 80g (3 oz) per portion)
4		small cloves garlic

NOODLES

1		medium red pimento
2		egg whites
2		egg yolks
350g	(12 oz)	flour
5g		salt
1 tsp		walnut or olive oil

SAUCE

		chopped bones from lamb
½		carrot, diced
½		onion, diced
approx 1 litre	(1¾ pints)	water
1		sprig fresh rosemary
1		small clove garlic, crushed
200ml	(1 cup)	cream
15g	(½ oz)	unsalted butter seasoning

MIXED NUT PITHIVIER

PASTRY: Cut the pastry into 2 pieces, 1 slightly larger than the other. Lightly dust a flat surface with flour and roll out the smaller piece. Cut out a 25cm (10″) diameter circle, about 2mm (1/16″) thick for the base. Place on a baking tray brushed with a little water.

Roll out the larger piece of pastry slightly thicker — approximately 3mm (1/8″) — and cut out a round piece the same size as the base. Put aside.

Brush the base with beaten egg.

FILLING: Place all the nuts in a food processor and process until well ground.

With a wooden spoon, beat the butter until soft, then work in the ground nuts, icing sugar and flour. Add the eggs one at a time and mix in. Spoon the nut cream mixture onto the base and spread to within 30mm (1″) of the edges, leaving an egg-washed rim around the filling. Place the top piece of puff pastry over the filling and firmly press the 2 pieces together to seal the edges. Do this by simply using your fingers: press down the edges with your middle and ring fingers, then, holding a small knife vertically, bring the pastry in between your fingers.

Brush the top completely with egg wash, then using the point of a small knife, score curved lines from the centre to the edge, being careful not to cut right through the pastry. Place in the refrigerator and rest for 30 minutes before baking.

CRÈME ANGLAISE: Place a small heavy-bottomed pot over medium heat. Pour in the milk and bring to the boil. Lower the heat. Place the egg yolks, sugar and frangelico in a bowl and beat well until the mixture turns a pale yellow. Pour in half the hot milk and mix together. Pour the egg mixture into the remaining milk and place over a gentle heat.

Stirring continuously with a wooden spoon, cook the mixture until it thickens enough to coat the back of the spoon.

Do not allow it to boil. Once cooked, pass it through a fine sieve into a clean bowl. Allow to cool, stirring from time to time. Cover with plastic wrap and put aside. Keep at room temperature.

PITHIVIER: Preheat an oven to 220°C (425°F) and bake the pithivier for 10 minutes. Lower the heat to 190°C (375°F) and bake a further 15–20 minutes. Remove from the oven and dust with icing sugar. Turn the grill onto high and very carefully, watching and turning the pithivier, glaze under the high heat, giving it a lovely shine. This takes only a few seconds so be careful not to burn it.

TO SERVE: A pithivier is best served warm, although it may also be served at room temperature. Cut it into 8 even portions.

Spoon a little frangelico crème anglaise onto each plate, place a slice of pithivier next to this, and serve.

Classically, a gâteau pithivier consists of sweet almond cream between two layers of puff pastry. Although we follow the same procedures as the classical recipe we have found that a combination of nuts rather than just almonds make a delicious gâteau. Add to this the velvety hazelnut liqueur-flavoured crème anglaise, and the result is mouthwatering.

The preparation is quite simple but to ensure success, care must be taken in sealing the two layers of pastry together. Also, allow the pastry to rest after each stage of preparation so it will keep its shape during baking.

INGREDIENTS — SERVES 8–12

500g	(1 lb)	Puff Pastry (see page 144)
		egg to glaze
		icing sugar to dust
		flour for rolling out pastry

MIXED NUT CREAM FILLING

55g	(2 oz)	hazelnuts
55g	(2 oz)	walnuts
55g	(2 oz)	almonds
85g	(3 oz)	butter
170g	(6 oz)	icing sugar
15g	(½ oz)	flour
2		small eggs

FRANGELICO CRÈME ANGLAISE

450ml	(2 cups)	milk
6		egg yolks
100g	(4 oz)	sugar
about 45ml	(3 tbsp)	frangelico

BROWN ONION SOUP

French Brown Onion Soup is a traditional favourite, topped with crisp slices of French bread covered in a gruyère or freshly grated parmesan. The addition of a heavy draught beer gives this soup yet another flavour dimension. The bite of the beer, along with the hops flavour, makes a very interesting combination.

INGREDIENTS — SERVES 6

500g	(1 lb)	red or brown onion
50g	(2 oz)	unsalted butter
1		small clove garlic, crushed
500ml	(2¼ cups)	heavy draught beer or stout
1 litre	(4½ cups)	Brown Beef Stock (see page 140)
½		bayleaf
½ tsp		fresh sage or pinch of dried sage
		ground pepper and salt

CROÛTONS

6		slices French bread
125g	(4 oz)	freshly grated gruyère or parmesan cheese
1 dsp		chopped parsley

METHOD: Peel the onions and cut them in half, then thinly slice across the onion. Melt the butter in a heavy-bottomed pot. Quickly sauté the garlic, then add the onions and cook over medium heat until they begin to brown. Stir regularly to ensure even browning. Add the beer, then the beef stock and the bayleaf. Bring to the boil and skim off any impurities. Add the sage. Simmer for 25 minutes over a gentle heat. Remove the bayleaf. Season to taste with ground pepper and salt.

CROÛTONS: Toast both sides of the bread under the grill. Butter one side then liberally sprinkle with cheese.

TO SERVE: Pour the soup into 6 soup bowls and place a cheese croûton on top. Sprinkle a little more cheese over the soup if you like. Place under a hot grill and melt the cheese.

Remove from the heat, sprinkle with chopped parsley, and serve while piping hot.

NEW ZEALAND WHITEBAIT TIMBALE

The original version of this dish won the New Zealand Master Chefs Association team a gold medal at the 1987 Salon Culinaire in Vancouver. The original dish was a main course, consisting of a whitebait timbale and a seafood ragoût with an American Sauce and an Avocado Beurre Blanc. We prepare it as an entrée, with a Chervil Beurre Blanc, but the main item remains the same.

METHOD: Chill 6 x 100ml (half-cup) moulds then brush them with soft butter.

Break the eggs into a bowl, add the lemon juice, nutmeg and cream, and mix together well. Strain through a fine sieve into another bowl. Add the zest and season to taste. Evenly divide the whitebait between the 6 buttered moulds; do not press down. Pour on the egg custard, filling each mould almost to the top. Brush 6 pieces of tinfoil with butter then cover each mould.

Lay a cloth in an ovenproof tray and place in the whitebait timbales. Pour in hot water to two-thirds the height of the moulds. Place in a preheated 150° C (300° F) oven for 40–45 minutes. Do not allow the water to boil.

Check the timbales occasionally during cooking time; when cooked, they should be set and able to withstand a delicate touch with your finger without breaking the surface layer. Remove from the oven and rest on the bench top for 5–10 minutes before turning out. Prepare the sauce during the cooking and resting time.

BEURRE BLANC: Place a pot over a gentle to medium heat, and add the diced shallots, white wine and vinegar. Reduce until almost all the liquid has evaporated. Add the fish stock and simmer for 2 minutes. Add the cream and mix together. Whisk in the butter, a piece at a time, continuing to whisk rapidly until all the butter is incorporated. Season to taste.

TO SERVE: Carefully turn the whitebait timbales out by lightly shaking the moulds until you feel them release. Place each in the centre of a warm plate.

Pass the beurre blanc through a fine sieve. Add the chervil. Check the seasoning and consistency. Spoon the sauce around the whitebait and serve immediately.

As a variation, small dice of mixed vegetables added to the beurre blanc just before serving adds flavour and colour.

INGREDIENTS — SERVES 6

WHITEBAIT TIMBALE

300g (11 oz)	whitebait
	butter for brushing moulds
3	eggs
	juice of 1 lemon
	pinch of nutmeg
100ml (½ cup)	cream
	zest of ½ a lemon, finely diced
	pepper and salt

CHERVIL BEURRE BLANC

4	small shallots, finely diced
100ml (½ cup)	dry white wine
50ml (3½ tbsp)	white wine vinegar
100ml (½ cup)	fish stock
25ml (2 tbsp)	cream
350g (12 oz)	unsalted butter, cut into small knobs
	pepper and salt
	fresh chervil

SPARKLING WINE AND LEMON GRANITE

Any good dry sparkling wine will do a fine job in this refreshing granite. I have to say, though, that champagne makes the best granite. If possible, even make this recipe with pink champagne. Remember a granite should resemble crushed ice.

INGREDIENTS — SERVES 6–8

75g (3 oz)	castor sugar
1 tsp	water
	juice of 2 lemons
½	bottle sparkling wine or champagne (brut)

METHOD: Bring the sugar, water and lemon juice slowly to the boil and simmer for 1 minute. Allow to cool.

Add the wine and mix well. Pass into a flat, freezer-proof tray and freeze. As the liquid begins to freeze at the the edges, give it a good stir. Repeat this process regularly, depending on how fine you want the ice crystals.

Once frozen and ready to serve, scrape up the granite with a spoon and serve it in champagne glasses or in small halves of lemon skin. Make sure the serving container is also well chilled. Serve immediately.

MARINATED HARE WITH CELERIAC

Hare is best eaten young, and its age can be assessed easily by checking a few obvious points.

A hare under one year (a leveret) has a white belly and pliable ears. Its claws are small and almost hidden under the paw fur. The fur should be soft and smooth. The signs of an old, and probably tough, hare are matted fur, yellow teeth and long claws. The best cut is the saddle on the back, which in a young animal can be served medium-rare. It should be cooked longer with older animals.

Hare usually tastes better when marinated, and we use the same cooked marinade for hare, rabbit and venison.

If you shoot your own hare, before eating hang it by the hind feet for 3 to 4 days. Clean and skin the hare, also removing the bluish layer of muscle that covers the saddle. Use the hindquarters and forequarters for stews, casseroles, etc.

METHOD: A day ahead, cover the hare meat in cooked marinade. Cover with plastic wrap and leave in the refrigerator.

PEARS: Peel the pears and core them from the side, making a cavity; leave the stalk on. Place the wine, vinegar, brown sugar, water, bayleaf and clove in a medium-sized pot. Bring to the boil. Add the pears, and cook until soft but not mushy. Allow to cool in the poaching liquid. Remove from the liquid when cool and drain on kitchen paper on a tray. Place in a lightly buttered ovenproof tray with a little poaching liquid. Cover with tinfoil and put aside.

CELERIAC MOUSSE: Peel the celeriac and cut it into 2cm (1″) pieces. Boil in plenty of salted water until tender (15–18 minutes). Drain well on kitchen paper, removing all excess water.

Melt the clarified butter in a small pan and sauté the finely diced shallot until tender; do not allow to colour.

Place the celeriac and shallot in a food processor and process until very smooth. Add the eggs and yolks as you go, to aid the processing. Push through a fine sieve into a clean bowl. Season to taste with pepper and salt, and add the cream.

Liberally brush 6 x 100ml (half-cup) moulds with butter and evenly divide the mousse between them. Cover with tinfoil and place in a bain marie with warm water to halfway up the sides of the moulds.

SAUCE: Combine the marinade, tomato paste and brown stock. Reduce over medium heat by two-thirds. Add the horseradish and simmer for 1 minute. Season to taste. Dilute the arrowroot with red wine and mix into the sauce. Simmer for 1–2 minutes. Pass through a fine sieve into a clean pot, and put aside.

COOKING AND SERVING: Place the mousses and the covered tray of pears in a medium oven and cook for 15–20 minutes.

Making sure it is well drained and seasoned, sauté the hare on all sides in hot clarified butter. Reduce the heat and continue to sauté for 8–10 minutes, or until medium rare. The time will vary with the size of your hare. Turn regularly.

Once cooked, remove the hare from the heat and rest for 5 minutes in a warm place. Heat the sauce to serving temperature, whisk in a knob of butter, and adjust the seasoning and consistency if necessary.

Turn out the celeriac mousses by running a small knife around the edge, then carefully shaking out. Place on hot plates; place a heated pear next to each mousse. Cut the hare saddles into 6 even portions and fan out from the celeriac mousse. Spoon over the sauce and garnish with fresh herbs.

Serve with carrots and courgette ribbons tossed in Beurre Battu or Beurre Fondue (see page 132) flowing out of the cavity in the pear.

Celeriac is a special variety of celery traditionally cultivated in Europe for its thick, tuberous root. Celeriac makes a lovely mousse to accompany hare, and combines well with pear or apple. When peeling and preparing celeriac, keep it in lemon water to keep it from going brown.

INGREDIENTS — SERVES 6

3		saddles of hare, sinews and bones removed cooked Marinade (see page 50)
50g	(2 oz)	clarified butter for sautéing

PEARS

6		small Winter Cole or other suitable pears
300ml	(1¼ cups)	red wine
50ml	(3½ tbsp)	red wine vinegar
100g	(4 oz)	brown sugar water to just cover
1		bayleaf
1		clove

CELERIAC MOUSSE

400g	(14 oz)	celeriac
15g	(½ oz)	clarified butter
1		shallot, finely diced
2		whole eggs and 2 yolks pepper and salt
75ml	(⅓ cup)	cream butter for brushing moulds

SAUCE

		Marinade, strained (see page 50)
1 tsp		tomato paste
400ml	(1¾ cups)	Brown Game Stock (see page 140)
½ tbsp		grated horseradish or horseradish cream pepper and salt
2g		arrowroot knob of butter

Occasionally a chef comes across a recipe that just cannot be passed by — one that needs no alteration to its already perfect state.

The following classic chocolate mousse recipe has to be one of the best ever: light and airy, yet distinctive in flavour. It is simple to prepare and results in a wonderful dessert.

RICH CHOCOLATE MOUSSE

INGREDIENTS — SERVES 6–8

200g	(7 oz)	plain chocolate
150ml	(⅔ cup)	cream
5		egg whites
75g	(3 oz)	castor sugar
2–3 dsp		granulated coffee
5		egg yolks
6–8		chocolate runouts (see glossary)
		fresh raspberries

METHOD: Chop or grate the chocolate into small pieces and place it in a large bowl over a water bath set over a medium heat. Stir occasionally until the chocolate is completely melted and smooth.

Lightly whip the cream and put it aside. In a separate bowl beat the egg whites to a stiff snow, adding two-thirds of the sugar as you go. Put aside.

Add the coffee, the remaining sugar and the egg yolks, and beat until the sugar and coffee have dissolved. Now you must keep the chocolate quite warm as the addition of the next ingredients will considerably cool it. Using a whisk, mix in the egg yolk and sugar mixture, then whisk in the beaten cream. Beat until evenly mixed, but do not overbeat or the mousse will lose volume. Immediately fold in the beaten egg white with a large spoon. Pour into 6–8 tall glasses and place in the refrigerator to set for at least 1 hour.

TO SERVE: Pipe a rosette of cream on the top of each mousse, sprinkle over some raspberries (or strawberries) and place a chocolate runout on top. Serve immediately.

TOMATO AND ARTICHOKE FLAN

On occasion a guest at Huka Lodge will request a no meat alternative to the day's menu. This menu consists of some of the vegetarian dishes we like to make.

For this dish we always use tinned artichoke bottoms. They are of good quality and reduce the rather complicated procedure of preparing fresh artichokes. Tinned artichoke hearts or bottoms are packed in brine so need to be rinsed before use. They are perfect for many cooked dishes.

METHOD: Lightly flour a flat surface and roll out the pastry to a thickness of approximately 4mm ($1/16$"). Lightly butter a 22cm (9") flan ring and place it on a baking sheet. Carefully line the flan ring with pastry, then with a circle of greaseproof paper, and fill with beans or rice. Place in the refrigerator to rest for 20–30 minutes, then blind bake in a preheated 175°C (350°F) oven for 20–25 minutes, or until golden brown around the rim.

Remove from the oven and allow to cool for 5 minutes. Remove the paper and beans. Increase the temperature to 200°C (400°F) and bake the flan case for a further 10 minutes. Remove from the heat and leave to cool to room temperature.

TOMATO: Blanch and seed the tomatoes. Roughly dice the flesh and place on kitchen paper to draw out some of the moisture. Season with pepper and salt and mix in the chopped parsley.

ARTICHOKE: Place the artichokes in a food processor and purée until smooth.

Dissolve the gelatine in warm vegetable stock then add it to the artichoke purée. Process for approximately 1 minute, then push through a fine sieve into a clean bowl. Cool. Lightly whip the cream then mix it into the purée. Season to taste.

Whisk the egg white to a fluffy snow then carefully fold in purée.

ASSEMBLY: Evenly spread the tomato over the bottom of the flan case; press down lightly. Pour over the artichoke purée and allow to set in the refrigerator.

TO SERVE: Once set, remove the flan carefully from the ring and slide it onto a cutting surface. Cut into even portions and serve with a tomato coulis or vinaigrette.

INGREDIENTS — SERVES 6–8

300g	(11 oz)	Short Pastry (see page 145)
4		large tomatoes, skinned and seeded
		pepper and salt
½ tbsp		chopped parsley
300g	(11 oz)	tinned artichoke bottoms
175ml	(¾ cup)	Vegetable Stock (see page 139)
4		gelatine leaves or 1 tbsp gelatine
150ml	(⅔ cup)	cream
1		egg white

Shiitake mushrooms originate in Japan where they grow on hardwood, usually oak. Their name is made up of the Japanese word for hardwood (shii) and the name of the mushrooms (take).

They are now grown in New Zealand and are available here fresh. They are also available dried from Japanese food shops. Fresh shiitakes are very delicate and in this recipe do not require cooking.

VEGETABLE POTAGE

METHOD: Melt the butter in a large pot, add the leek, carrot, onion and celery, and cook over a gentle heat with the lid on. Add the tomato paste, mix together and continue to cook for 2 minutes with the lid on.

Remove the lid. Add the stock and bring to the boil, skimming off all impurities as they rise. Lower the heat to a gentle simmer. Add the potato and bayleaf, and simmer gently for 30–40 minutes.

Once cooked, remove the bayleaf. Place in a liquidiser or food processor and process until smooth, then push through a medium sieve into a clean pot. Season to taste and correct the consistency if necessary. Thinly slice the shiitake mushrooms and put aside until required.

CROÛTONS: Cut the slice of bread into even cubes. Heat the clarified butter in a frypan then sauté the cubes until golden on all sides. Toss regularly to ensure even browning. Drain on kitchen paper.

TO SERVE: Bring the soup to serving temperature. Add the cream, chopped parsley and thyme. Evenly divide the shiitake between 6 hot soup bowls, and pour over the hot soup. Sprinkle with a few croutons and garnish with a sprig of chervil. Serve with French bread.

INGREDIENTS — SERVES 6

50g (2 oz)	unsalted butter
100g (4 oz)	leek, washed and chopped
150g (5 oz)	carrot, peeled and chopped
100g (4 oz)	onion, peeled and sliced
100g (4 oz)	celery, washed and chopped
½ tbsp	tomato paste
1500ml (2½ pints)	strong Vegetable Stock (see page 139)
200g (7 oz)	potato, washed, peeled and chopped
1	small bayleaf
1	small clove garlic, crushed
200ml (1 cup)	cream
1 tsp	chopped parsley
1 tsp	chopped thyme pepper and salt

GARNISH

6	medium-sized shiitake mushrooms
1	slice of bread
50g (2 oz)	clarified butter
6	sprigs chervil

TOMATO AND BASIL SORBET

There are many savoury sorbets. The one we find most refreshing is this tomato and basil sorbet. Be sure to use ripe tomatoes.

INGREDIENTS — SERVES 6

25g	(1 oz)	sugar
200ml	(1 cup)	water
4		ripe tomatoes, skinned and seeded
1 tbsp		chopped basil
1 tsp		worcestershire sauce
		ground pepper
		pinch of salt
		juice of 1 lemon

METHOD: Dissolve the sugar in the water, add all the other ingredients and process until smooth in a liquidiser or food processor. Freeze in an ice cream machine, or in a bowl in the freezer, stirring regularly to achieve an even texture.

TO SERVE: Serve in hollowed out tomato halves or small chilled glasses, and garnish with a fresh basil leaf.

VEGETARIAN STRUDEL

This strudel is made using filo pastry, which dries out very quickly once exposed to the air. It is therefore important to prepare all the vegetables first and organise the ingredients so the strudel can be constructed quickly. The vegetables inside can be varied according to taste; any number of combinations are possible.

INGREDIENTS — SERVES 6

100g	(4 oz)	green beans
150g	(5 oz)	carrot buttons
125g	(4 oz)	or 1 bunch spinach
4		medium-sized tomatoes
100g	(4 oz)	button mushrooms
1		medium-sized avocado
		lemon juice
50g	(2 oz)	butter
6		squares of filo, 2 layers thick
50g	(2 oz)	pine nuts
		pepper and salt
20g	(1 oz)	parmesan

SAUCE

1		shallot, finely diced
1		clove garlic, crushed
25g	(1 oz)	butter
200g	(7 oz)	pumpkin, peeled and finely diced
1 tsp		tomato purée
500ml	(2¼ cups)	Vegetable Stock (see page 139)
		pinch of nutmeg
		seasoning
50ml	(3½ tbsp)	cream (optional)

METHOD: Trim and wash the beans and blanch them in plenty of boiling salted water. Cut the carrots into buttons and blanch. Wash and trim the spinach, quickly blanch and squeeze dry.

Plunge the tomatoes into boiling water for 3 seconds then straight into cold water. Skin the tomatoes then cut them into quarters; remove the seeds. Put the flesh aside ready for use with the other vegetables.

Wash and slice the mushrooms. Peel the avocado and slice it into strips; brush it with lemon juice to prevent it going brown. Melt the butter.

FILO: Unroll the filo pastry and separate it into 2-layer piles. Brush the top with melted butter then cut it into squares of the required size.

TO ASSEMBLE: Starting 8cm (3″) in from the end closest to you, lay a row of avocado the width of the filo, starting and finishing 4cm (1½″) from each side. Sprinkle over some of the pine nuts, then fold over the end and brush with melted butter.

Next lay the beans and tomato in a row the same way. Season. Begin to roll up, folding the avocado over the beans and tomato. Brush the exposed filo with melted butter. Repeat this process with the remaining vegetables, finally rolling a layer of filo around the whole package. Tuck under each end. Brush with butter and sprinkle with grated parmesan. Place on a lightly buttered baking sheet ready for baking. Repeat with the remaining 5 strudels.

PUMPKIN SAUCE: Place the shallot, garlic and butter in a pot over medium heat. Sauté until tender. Do not allow to colour. Add the pumpkin and tomato purée and mix together. Add all the remaining ingredients except the cream.

Cook until the pumpkin is tender, then place in a liquidiser and process until smooth. Pass through a medium sieve into a clean bowl. Season to taste. Put aside until required.

COOKING AND SERVING: Cook the strudels in a preheated 250° C (475° F) oven for 15–20 minutes.

Heat the sauce to serving temperature, add the cream. Remove the strudels from the oven, cut in half and place on warmed plates. Spoon on the pumpkin sauce. Garnish with fresh herbs and serve immediately.

PEPPERED PINEAPPLE

Use fresh pineapple for this dish, as nothing beats its full, fragrant flavour.

When purchasing, avoid any pineapples that are bruised or have a wilting stalk and leaves. Avoid pineapples that do not have a fragrant scent and are very unripe, as they will never fully ripen.

METHOD: Top and tail the pineapple, then with a sharp knife carefully cut away the outer skin. With the point of a sharp knife or peeler scoop out any brown pits. Lay the pineapple on its side and slice 6 pieces approximately 15mm (½″) thick. With a plain pastry cutter stamp out the hard core and discard.

Liberally grind black pepper over both sides of each piece of pineapple. Place on a tray and put aside until required.

FRUIT: Hull the strawberries and cut into halves or quarters depending on their size. Scoop out melon balls using a medium–sized scoop. Peel the kiwifruit, cut them in half, then cut each half into 3 wedges.

ORANGE SAUCE: Add the orange juice to the sugar syrup and bring to the boil. Skim if necessary.

Dilute the arrowroot with the nip of cointreau or grand marnier. Whisk into the syrup, then with a wooden spoon stir back to the boil. Reduce the heat and simmer for 2 minutes.

Blanch the orange zest in water for 10 minutes. Pass the sauce through a fine sieve into a clean bowl and add the zest. Cover with plastic wrap and allow to cool.

TO SERVE: Place a pineapple ring in the centre of each chilled plate.

Mix all the fruit together except the apple, and toss in a little of the orange sauce. Spoon the fruit into the middle of each peppered pineapple ring.

Evenly pour the remaining sauce around each, and garnish with fresh apple and mint. Serve with Orange Tuiles (see page 71).

INGREDIENTS — SERVES 6

1	medium-sized pineapple
	ground pepper
18	strawberries
18	melon balls
2	kiwifruit
24	raspberries
1	apple
	fresh mint to garnish

ORANGE SAUCE

300ml (1¼ cups)	Sugar Syrup (see page 146)
	juice of 3 oranges
30ml (2 tbsp)	cointreau or grand marnier
5g (2½ level tsp)	arrowroot or cornflour
	zest of 1 orange

DUCK PÂTÉ

In making any form of pâté, the quality and freshness of the base ingredients are of the utmost importance.

Wild ducks may be used for this pâté if available, otherwise Peking or Aylesbury are suitable; fresh is always better than frozen and free-range better than battery.

To test the freshness of a duck, make sure the underbill can be bent back easily and the webbing is pliable. For commercially obtained ducks pinch the breast, which should feel meaty. Hang wild ducks by their feet for 6 to 7 days before drawing and plucking.

To ensure the pâté remains moist the mould is lined with thinly sliced pork fat. To do this, semi-freeze the piece of fat then carefully slice it with a sharp knife or on a bacon slicer. Bacon can also be used in the same way.

INGREDIENTS — SERVES 12–15

1		whole medium to large duck
200g	(7 oz)	lean pork
150g	(5 oz)	pork fat
150g	(5 oz)	duck or chicken livers, marinated in a little port and brandy
½ tsp		chopped sage
1		small clove of garlic, crushed
½ tsp		mixed spice
8		black peppercorns, crushed
		juice of 1 orange
		zest of ½ orange
1		finely diced shallot
1 tbsp		armagnac
2 tbsp	(3 tbsp)	brandy
50g	(2 oz)	pistachio nuts, shelled
50g	(2 oz)	chopped truffle (optional)
		pepper and salt
300g	(11 oz)	thinly sliced pork fat

METHOD: Remove the breasts from the duck and trim, leaving the skin on. Put aside. Joint the remainder of the duck, and remove all bone, skin and ligaments. Cut up the duck (except the breasts), pork meat and pork fat.

Place the meat in a bowl, keeping the fat separate. Add the sage, garlic, spice, black pepper, orange juice and zest, shallot, and all the alcohol.

Mix together then cover with tinfoil and marinate for 24 hours in the refrigerator. Stir occasionally.

Marinate the livers for the same period.

Soak the pistachios in hot water until the skin is easily removed. Put aside until required.

Drain the marinating liquid off the meat and livers. Mince the meat twice through a fine mincer and the fat once, then mix together. Keep the forcemeat cold at all times.

Heat a little clarified butter in a large frypan and quickly sauté the livers until browned. Pat dry and allow to cool. Cut the livers into pieces then mix into the forcemeat.

Quickly seal and brown the duck breasts. Allow to cool. Mix the shelled pistachios and chopped truffle into the forcemeat. Season to taste with pepper and salt.

Line a terrine with slices of pork fat or bacon. Half fill the terrine with forcemeat and lay in the duck breasts. If necessary cut the breasts in half lengthways to ensure they reach the length of the terrine. Top up with the remaining forcemeat. Fold over the excess fat or bacon then lay a couple of pieces of pork fat or bacon along the top.

Cover the pâté with tinfoil or a lid and place in a deep roasting tray. Two-thirds fill with hot water and place in a preheated oven at 190°C (375°F) for 1 hour. The temperature should be regulated to ensure the water stays at a gentle simmer.

Once cooked, allow the pâté to cool completely overnight before turning out.

TO SERVE: Briefly dip the terrine in hot water and carefully remove the pâté. Slice it into portions and serve with warm Cumberland Sauce (see page 113), salad, toast or toasted brioche. Well covered, the pâté will keep several days in the refrigerator.

ROCK LOBSTER BISQUE

METHOD: Melt 25g (1 oz) butter in a heavy-bottomed pot. Add the vegetables and garlic, and lightly cook without allowing to colour. Add the tomato paste and cook for a further minute. Add the flour; cook for 2 minutes. Add the shells, mix together and cook for 2 minutes, then add the wine and brandy and cook for a further 3 minutes. Add the cold fish stock and mix together, then add the bayleaf. Bring to the boil, stirring regularly to ensure nothing is sticking to the bottom of the pot. Skim off any impurities as they rise. Lower the heat and simmer for 20 minutes.

Pass through a very fine sieve into a clean pot, to ensure all pieces of shell, etc., are removed. Season to taste with pepper and salt. Put aside until required.

PASTRY STICKS: Roll out the puff pastry to a thickness of approximately 1mm. Brush with egg-wash and sprinkle with the cayenne pepper and paprika. Cut into 6 strips approximately 1cm (½″) wide and 12cm (5″) long. Twist the end in opposite directions (like a Christmas decoration) then place on a baking sheet, pressing down each end so the shape is held. Bake in a hot oven until golden brown. Remove from the heat and store in an airtight container until required.

TO SERVE: Heat the bisque to serving temperature. Add the cream then whisk in a knob of butter. Do not boil. Check the seasoning. Pour into 6 hot soup bowls. Place a swirl of cream on the top of each and garnish with a sprig of chervil. Serve with spicy pastry sticks.

This soup is an excellent way to use up rock lobster or crayfish shells and bodies after you have enjoyed the flesh from the tail. The remaining body and shell can be frozen until required.

The spicy pastry sticks are made from puff pastry trimmings and offcuts.

INGREDIENTS — SERVES 6

25g	(1 oz)	butter
1		medium-sized carrot, peeled and sliced
1		medium-sized onion, peeled and sliced
100g	(4 oz)	celery, sliced
1		clove garlic, crushed
1 tbsp		tomato paste
25g	(1 oz)	flour
500–600g	(1–1¼ lb)	crayfish or lobster shell, roughly crushed
100ml	(½ cup)	white wine
50ml	(3½ tbsp)	brandy
1500ml	(2½ pints)	Fish Stock (see page 139)
1		bayleaf
		pepper and salt
100ml	(½ cup)	cream, plus 6 tbsp for garnish
		knob unsalted butter
6		sprigs chervil

SPICY PASTRY STICKS

offcuts of puff pastry
egg-wash
pinch of cayenne
pinch of paprika

If the babaco is very ripe, reduce the amount of sugar to 50g.

BABACO AND LIME SORBET

INGREDIENTS — SERVES 6

350ml	(1½ cups)	water
100g	(4 oz)	sugar
400g	(14 oz)	ripe babaco
		juice of 2 limes
		finely diced zest of ½
		lime

METHOD: Boil the water and sugar together. Simmer for 3 minutes. Allow to cool completely.

Purée the babaco then pass it through a sieve into a clean bowl. Add the lime juice and zest. Pour on the sugar syrup and mix together.

Freeze immediately in a sorbetière or in the freezer, whisking regularly to achieve a smooth texture.

Serve in a hollowed out half-lime skin or in an elegant chilled glass.

LAMB IN A HERB CRUST

This dish is usually done using strip loin of lamb or saddle, but it may be adapted to chops and cutlets.

LAMB: Mix the herbs, brioche crumbs, spice and ground pepper together. Place in a flat container.

Heat the clarified butter in a large frypan, season the lamb then brown it on all sides in the hot butter. Dry and allow to cool.

Roll the lamb in flour, then shake off the excess. Dip it into the beaten egg white, shake off the excess liquid then roll it in the prepared herbs. Carefully but firmly pat the herb coating down to achieve an even, all-over covering. Cover and put in a cool place until required.

JUS: Roughly chop the vegetables and sauté them with the rosemary and garlic until lightly browned.

Place the lamb bones and trimmings in a hot oven and roast until well browned. Do not burn. Once done, drain off the excess fat and place over a high heat. Add the port and bayleaf and simmer for 2 minutes. Transfer to a heavy-bottomed pot with browned vegetables and add the veal stock. Over a medium heat reduce by two-thirds, skimming off all impurities as they rise.

Blanch the orange zest in a little water. Place the orange juice and honey together in a small pot over a medium to high heat and carefully reduce to an amber syrup. Watch carefully so as not to over-brown or burn.

Pass the reduced stock through a fine sieve onto the honey and orange syrup and mix together over a gentle heat until totally combined. Season with a little pepper and salt to taste then cover and put aside until required.

COOKING THE LAMB: Melt a little clarified butter in a pan, add the lamb, then roast in a preheated oven at 190°C (375°F) for approximately 10 minutes. Turn the lamb regularly so that it colours evenly and the herb crust does not overcook on one side. Remove the lamb from the oven and leave it to rest 5 minutes in a warm place before cutting. Do not cover or the crust will become soft and soggy.

TO SERVE: Heat the jus to serving temperature, whisk in a knob of unsalted butter then add the blanched orange zest. Check the seasoning.

Carefully slice the lamb into medallions and divide into 6 even portions. Arrange on 6 hot plates then pour the hot jus around the lamb. Garnish with a sprig of fresh rosemary.

The lamb may be accompanied by Sautéed Eggplant (see page 129), snow peas and Marquise Potatoes (see page 135).

AN ALTERNATIVE: Cut the lamb into medallions, beat out a little with a meat hammer, then coat in crust. Sauté in clarified butter over medium heat until golden brown. Serve as opposite.

INGREDIENTS – SERVES 6

10g	(½ oz)	rosemary, finely chopped
20g	(1 oz)	parsley, finely chopped
10g	(½ oz)	marjoram, finely chopped
40g	(2 oz)	brioche crumbs
1		pinch Chinese 5 spice powder
		ground black pepper
		clarified butter
600g	(1¼ lb)	lamb strip loin, trimmed of all fat and sinew
		salt
		flour for coating
2–3		egg whites, lightly beaten

ORANGE AND HONEY JUS

1		medium-sized carrot
½		medium-sized onion
50g	(2 oz)	sliced leek
1		sprig fresh rosemary, chopped
1		small clove garlic, crushed
		all trimmings and any bones from the lamb, chopped
200ml	(1 cup)	madeira port
1 litre	(4½ cups)	Brown Veal Stock (see page 140)
		zest of 1 orange
		juice of 3 oranges
1 tbsp		liquid honey
		seasoning
		knob of unsalted butter

Syllabub is an old English dessert; it is thickened by the acid in the lemon juice coagulating the cream. A syllabub should be very light and just lemony enough to avoid being over-rich.

WHISKY AND WALNUT SYLLABUB

INGREDIENTS — SERVES 6–8

100g	(4 oz)	castor sugar
about 45ml	(3 tbsp)	whisky
60ml	(4 tbsp)	sweet white wine (e.g. late harvest Rhine Riesling)
600ml	(2½ cups)	cream
		juice of 2 lemons
3		finely chopped walnuts

GARNISH

	whipped cream
3	walnuts, halved
	grated chocolate (optional)

METHOD: Dissolve the sugar in the whisky and wine. Place the cream in a bowl and lightly whisk.

Add the lemon juice and the whisky-wine mixture to the cream a little at a time, mixing together well as the cream thickens. Do not over-beat. Carefully mix in the finely chopped walnuts.

Pour into 6 martini glasses. Cover with plastic film and place in the refrigerator for 2 hours before serving.

TO SERVE: Pipe on a rosette of cream, then place a walnut on top. Sprinkle with grated chocolate if desired. Serve chilled.

SMOKED SALMON WITH QUAIL EGGS AND CAVIAR

Smoked salmon is expensive, therefore you want the best product for your money. Buy pale golden-pink smoked salmon; a deep golden orange colour could mean overcured and dry fish.

Slice the salmon paper-thin with a very sharp, thin-bladed, flexible knife. Cut across the fillet, working from the tail end backward, angling the knife slightly, blade edge towards the tail. I recommend removing any bones with a small pair of electrical pliers or tweezers before slicing.

Quail eggs are small, with a speckled shell; the shell should be uncracked, smooth and matt. They should feel heavy for their size in your hand, proving the air chamber in the egg is still small. The older the egg, the larger the air chamber gets, as the egg loses moisture through its pores. If unsure, once you get home, test the egg's freshness by placing it in cold water. If it floats, the egg is old. If it stays horizontal and immersed, it is fresh.

Beluga or sevruga caviar are best, but they are very expensive. The alternative is lumpfish roe or German or Danish caviar . . . nice, quite inexpensive, but nowhere near as good as the real thing.

QUAIL EGGS: Carefully crack the egg shell with the back of a small vegetable knife, then very carefully cut through the membrane just under the shell with the point of the knife. Part the shell and drop the egg into a small bowl with a little vinegar in it. Repeat with all the eggs.

Bring enough salted water to the boil to just cover the eggs. Lower the heat to a gentle simmer. Carefully swirl the pot of water so the water whirls inside. Tip all the eggs and vinegar in at once and continue to swirl, so that the eggs roll as they cook, thus forming a nice even rugby ball shape. Once the egg white has set, stop the movement and poach to a soft, slightly runny yolk. Carefully remove from the heat and immerse in cold water until required.

SALAD: Wash and dry the salad leaves. Place them in a bowl and sprinkle with the walnut oil, pepper and salt. Toss to ensure even coating.

SALMON: Thinly slice the salmon and arrange it evenly on chilled plates.

TO SERVE: Arrange the salad leaves on the plate of salmon. Add the quail eggs, and spoon on the caviar. Garnish with fresh dill and serve with lemon and brown bread.

INGREDIENTS — SERVES 6

12	quail eggs
	a little vinegar
	salad leaves (butterhead, red oak lettuce, endive, etc.)
	walnut oil
	salt and ground pepper
300 – 450g (¾ –1 lb)	smoked salmon (allow 50–75g (2–3 oz) per portion)
6 tsp	caviar or lumpfish roe
	dill, to garnish

This soup can be prepared using flour as a thickening agent, as in this recipe, or as a vegetable purée using the bulk of the contents and the possible addition of potato. In both cases the spinach is added last and cooking is only continued for further 5 minutes to retain the colour and goodness of the spinach.

SPINACH SOUP

INGREDIENTS — SERVES 6

25g	(1 oz)	butter
1		medium-sized onion, sliced
50g	(2 oz)	leek, chopped
1		medium to large clove of garlic, crushed
25g	(1 oz)	flour
2		pinches of grated nutmeg
1200ml	(2 pints)	Chicken Stock (see page 138)
350g	(12 oz)	blanched and squeezed out spinach
		salt and ground pepper
6 dsp		plain unsweetened yoghurt
1 tbsp		chopped mixed herbs

METHOD: Heat the butter in a pot, add the onion, leek and garlic, and cook until soft. Do not allow to colour. Add the flour and nutmeg, and cook over a gentle heat for 2 minutes.

Add the cold chicken stock and mix together, stirring until smooth. Cook until the liquid thickens, stirring from time to time. Add the spinach, cook a further 5 minutes, then remove from the heat. Liquidise and pass through a medium sieve into a clean pot. Season to taste with ground pepper and salt.

Mix the herbs with the yoghurt and season to taste.

TO SERVE: Heat the soup to serving temperature, then add the cream. Check the seasoning.

Pour into 6 hot soup bowls then spoon on a swirl of herb yoghurt. Serve while hot.

CUCUMBER SORBET

In recent years cucumber has become increasingly popular in sauces and sorbets. I prefer the telegraph or continental cucumber, which has fewer pips and a more tender skin. Whichever variety you purchase, they are best when young and juicy.

METHOD: Place the cucumber in a liquidiser and process until smooth. Pass through a fine sieve into a clean bowl, pushing as much of the pulp through as possible. Add all the other ingredients and mix together.

Pour into a sorbetière and process, or place in a large bowl in the freezer, whisking regularly to achieve a smooth texture.

TO SERVE: Serve in chilled glass or cucumber boats with a sprig of fresh mint.

INGREDIENTS — SERVES 6

1	medium-sized cucumber, skinned and seeded
	juice of 1 lemon
½ tsp	finely chopped mint
200ml (1 cup)	Sugar Syrup (see page 146)

Basil Sauce or Pesto is traditionally made with basil, pine nuts, parmesan and olive oil, and can be used added to sauces and salad dressings.

In this recipe we reduced the amount of oil and made a thick paste, which is used as a filling for the chicken.

Caul fat or crépinette is a spiderweb-like fatty membrane and is totally edible. It makes a perfect and, once cooked, invisible wrapping for many stuffed and sautéed or roasted meat dishes. Any good butcher will get it for you.

BREAST OF CHICKEN WITH PESTO

INGREDIENTS — SERVES 6

6	chicken breasts, with wing bone and skin
	pepper and salt
	clarified butter
6	sheets of caul fat (crépinette) about 12cm (5″) square

PESTO

150g (5 oz)	fresh basil
150g (5 oz)	grated parmesan
70g (3 oz)	pine nuts
3	small cloves garlic
½ tbsp	olive oil
	seasoning

SAUCE

1	medium-sized shallot, diced
60ml (4 tbsp)	brandy
500ml (2¼ cups)	Chicken Stock (see page 138)
50ml (3 tbsp)	meat Demi-Glaze (see page 141)
300ml (1¼ cups)	cream
	pepper and salt
	knob unsalted butter

PESTO: Blend together the basil, parmesan, pine nuts and garlic in a food processor until smooth. Add the oil and season to taste. Put aside until required.

CHICKEN: Trim and clean the wing bone down to the first joint. Leave the breast whole, with the skin on.

Carefully release the skin on one side only, and push the pesto evenly under the skin. Try to spread the pesto along the whole length of the breast, but do not overfill. Wrap each breast in one layer of caul fat then trim off any excess.

Season the chicken breasts on both sides with pepper and salt.

Heat the clarified butter in a large frypan and quickly brown both sides of the chicken breasts in hot butter. Do 1 or 2 breasts at a time to ensure the pan does not lose too much heat all at once.

Place the chicken right way up in a suitable roasting dish and cook in a preheated 190° C (375° F) oven for 10 minutes, or until the chicken is just slightly underdone. Rest for a further 10 minutes in a warm place.

SAUCE: While the chicken is resting, prepare the sauce. Place the diced shallot and brandy in a pan. Cook for 1 minute, add the chicken stock and reduce by two-thirds over medium heat. Add the meat glaze and cook for 1 minute. Add the cream, lower the heat and simmer until the sauce just begins to thicken.

TO SERVE: Pass the sauce through a fine sieve into a clean pot. Season to taste. Whisk in a knob of butter. The consistency may be corrected with a little chicken stock if it is too thick.

Cut each chicken and pesto breast once across and place it on a hot plate. Pour brandy sauce on and around the chicken and serve hot with blanched spinach, potato balls and Vegetable Spaghetti (see page 129).

VANILLA CREAMS IN APPLE CARAMEL

This dessert is our variation of a dish produced by the great French chef Georges Blanc in his restaurant La Mere Blanc, in the town of Vonnas. Blanc is probably the youngest chef in the world to be awarded the coveted 3 stars from Michelin for absolute excellence.

CARAMEL: Place the sugar and 100ml (half a cup) of the apple juice in a heavy-bottomed saucepan over high heat; cook until a rich caramel is reached. Keep a careful watch over the caramel as it will become bitter if overcooked; stand by with some extra apple juice to halt the caramelising process if necessary. Be very careful when adding liquid to hot caramel as there can be quite a violent reaction.

Allow the caramel to cool slightly then pour a little into the bottom of 6–8 x 100ml (half-cup) moulds. Return the remaining caramel to the heat and add the remaining 100ml (half-cup) of juice. Mix together then cover and allow to cool completely. Add extra apple juice if necessary to achieve a runny consistency once cold.

CUSTARD: Pour the milk and cream into a small saucepan and add the vanilla pod. Bring to the boil over medium heat.

Beat the eggs and sugar together, then add the calvados. Pour the hot milk and cream onto the eggs and mix well, then pass through a fine sieve into a clean bowl. Remove any froth. Fill each mould with custard.

Place a teatowel in the bottom of a small baking dish to prevent the moulds from moving around. Put in the filled moulds, and add hot water until it reaches halfway up the moulds. Cook in a preheated oven at 120–150° C (250–300° F) for approximately 30 minutes. Once set, remove from the heat and allow to cool.

TO SERVE: Loosen the edges of the caramels with your fingers. Tip upside down over a small plate and shake firmly to loosen the caramels from the moulds. Turn out onto cold plates.

Garnish with thinly sliced apple then pour the reserved apple caramel all around the custard. Garnish with fresh mint and serve.

INGREDIENTS — SERVES 6–8

400ml	(1¾ cups)	milk
100ml	(½ cup)	cream
1		vanilla pod
100g	(4 oz)	castor sugar
4		eggs
3		egg yolks
30ml	(2 tbsp)	calvados (optional)

CARAMEL

110g	(4 oz)	sugar
200ml	(1 cup)	clear apple juice

Bortsch or Bortschschock is the Russian national soup. There is, however, a Polish variation called Bortsch Polski. The Polish variation differs in that the stock used to prepare the bortsch is strongly flavoured with duck. There is always a roast duck garnish in the soup as well.

Both Russian and Polish Bortsch are coloured by the juices of red beetroot and served with sour cream. Bortsch is as good chilled as it is hot.

INGREDIENTS — SERVES 6

1		small duck
2 litres	(3½ pints)	Beef Stock (see page 140)
25g	(1 oz)	butter
2		raw beetroot, chopped
100g	(4 oz)	thinly sliced white cabbage
100g	(4 oz)	leeks, thinly sliced
100g	(4 oz)	onions, thinly sliced
100g	(4 oz)	celery, chopped
1		small carrot, chopped
1		bayleaf
1		sprig thyme
1 tsp		sugar
60ml	(4 tbsp)	red wine
2 tbsp	(3 tbsp)	red wine vinegar
		pepper and salt

GARNISH

1		cooked beetroot, julienned
100g	(4 oz)	cabbage
6 tbsp	(8 tbsp)	sour cream
		grated nutmeg
6		sprigs parsley

BORTSCH WITH ROAST DUCK

METHOD: Remove the breasts and thigh meat from the duck, trim and bone. Chop up the remaining duck carcass and cook it in a hot oven until quite brown.

Sauté the breast and thigh meat in hot butter or oil, then roast in the oven until done. Put aside once cooked.

Place the browned duck bones in a large pot, and pour over the beef stock. Bring to the boil, skim, then simmer gently for 15–20 minutes.

Melt 25g (1 oz) butter in another pot, add all the vegetables and sweat for 10 minutes, until the vegetables are tender but not browned. Strain the duck-flavoured stock onto the vegetables, add the herbs, sugar, wine and vinegar, then simmer gently for 45 minutes, skimming when necessary.

Thinly slice the roasted duck meat and the cooked beetroot for the garnish; blanch and dice the cabbage. Put aside ready for serving.

Once the bortsch is cooked, pass it through a fine sieve into a clean pot. Season to taste.

TO SERVE: Heat the bortsch to serving temperature. Evenly divide the duck meat, cabbage and beetroot between 6 hot soup bowls. Pour over the bortsch. Spoon on a tablespoon of sour cream then grate over a little nutmeg. Garnish with a parsley sprig and serve.

NOTE: If you are serving the bortsch chilled, follow the above process but chill the soup once you have strained it.

SALMON FEUILLETÉ

Feuilleté refers to dishes made with puff pastry as one of the main ingredients. This dish also uses saffron threads, which are the stigmas from a type of crocus. Each saffron crocus has only 3 stigmas and they are hand picked and dried. They are red-gold in colour and make a yellow sauce.

Although expensive, saffron is very strong and only a pinch is required for most dishes. There is a saffron powder available but it is of a lesser quality than the threads.

Saffron is important in Spanish cuisine and is popular in the South of France. It goes very well with many seafood dishes and soups.

INGREDIENTS — SERVES 6

1		fillet fresh salmon, skinned and boned (approx. 250g: 9 oz)
300g	(11 oz)	puff pastry
1		egg for egg-wash
		clarified butter
		pepper and salt

SAUCE

1		pinch saffron threads
200ml	(1 cup)	dry white wine
1		shallot, finely diced
		tomato trimmings from blanched tomato used as garnish
25ml	(2 tbsp)	white wine vinegar
200ml	(1 cup)	Fish Stock (see page 139)
200ml	(1 cup)	cream
100g	(4 oz)	butter
		pepper and salt

GARNISH

1		medium-sized tomato, blanched and seeded then diced
12		small fennel sprigs

METHOD: Roll out the puff pastry to a thickness of 4mm ($^1/_{16}''$) then carefully, without cutting into the pastry, score a crisscross pattern on the top. Rest in the refrigerator for 15 minutes. Cut out 6 shapes; stars, hearts, circles or squares. Beat the egg with a little water then brush each pastry shape with a little egg-wash.

Place on a baking sheet and rest for a further 10 minutes in the refrigerator. This will prevent the pastry from overshrinking during cooking.

Sprinkle a little water over the tray, then cook the pastry in a preheated oven at 200°C (400°F) for approximately 8 minutes.

Remove the feuilletés from the heat once cooked, and while warm carefully separate each into 3 layers, keeping each portion together, so as not to mix up shapes and sizes if there is a slight variation. If necessary, return the middle layer to the oven to dry out. Place on a cooling rack and put aside until required.

SAUCE: Place the saffron threads in the white wine and soak for 5–10 minutes. Place the shallot, tomato trimmings, vinegar, white wine and saffron and fish stock in a pot. Place over a medium to high heat and reduce by three-quarters, until quite a thick syrup remains.

Add the cream, lower the heat and gently simmer until the sauce just begins to thicken. Pass into a clean pot, cover to prevent a skin from forming and put aside until required.

SALMON: Slice the salmon into thin escalopes with a sharp, thin-bladed knife. Allow 3 escalopes per portion. Lightly season on both sides.

Heat the clarified butter in a large frypan over a medium to high heat. Make sure the butter is quite hot so the fish won't stick to the pan and so that it browns very quickly. Quickly sauté 2 or 3 pieces of salmon at a time, browning on both sides but not overcooking the fish. Once lightly and quickly browned, place it on a lightly buttered baking sheet and place in a medium oven for approximately 3 minutes, depending on its thickness. The salmon should be just slightly undercooked inside. Overcooking will result in dried out fish.

Heat the sauce then whisk in the butter, season to taste and add the diced tomato.

Heat the precooked feuilletés in the oven briefly, until warmed through.

TO SERVE: Carefully separate each feuilleté, place the base of each on a hot plate then put on 2 pieces of cooked fish and spoon on a little sauce. Carefully place the middle layer of pastry on top then the remaining piece of fish and again spoon on just a little sauce. Add the top of the feuilleté, then evenly divide the remaining sauce between each dish. Garnish with the fennel and serve hot.

CITRUS GRANITE

For this very refreshing granite we like to use limes, lemons and grapefruit, although you can also use oranges.

METHOD: Bring all the juice and the sugar to the boil in a small pot. Pass into a flat container and allow to freeze.

As the liquid begins to freeze, stir occasionally, depending on how fine you want the granules. Remember a granite should resemble crushed ice.

Segment the required amount of fruit and chill.

TO SERVE: This granite may be served in a half-lime or lemon shell or in a chilled glass.

Place a mixture of fruit segments in each glass.

Spoon in the citrus granite, garnish with mint and serve immediately.

INGREDIENTS — SERVES 6

150g (5 oz)	castor sugar
100ml (½ cup)	lemon juice
100ml (½ cup)	lime juice
200ml (1 cup)	grapefruit juice or orange
12	segments of each fruit

Gnocchi is the name given to a small Italian type of dumpling, which ranges in size from a large pea to about the size of a walnut. Traditionally, gnocchi are served with a grated cheese sauce.

For this dish, potato gnocchi are used. They may be poached in stock or salted water, or sautéed until a light golden colour. I have also chosen to change the shape, and we use a 4cm plain pastry cutter and cut out little discs. This way they are easier to handle and cook. We serve two each on top of the tournedos.

The sauce is dark and rich and goes well with beef and gnocchi.

Generally we choose prime cuts of beef, but this dish is just as tasty using other cuts such as sirloin, rump, or even a stewing steak.

INGREDIENTS — SERVES 6

6x100g (4 oz)	beef fillets, tied to keep their shape
	ground pepper and salt
	clarified butter
	well-flavoured beef stock, enough to cover the steaks

SAUCE

1	medium-sized onion
300ml (1¼ cups)	guinness
1 dsp	tomato purée
	pinch of brown sugar
800ml (3½ cups)	strongly flavoured Brown Beef Stock (see page 140)
½	bayleaf
1	sprig of thyme
2g (¾–1 level tsp)	arrowroot
	pepper and salt
	knob unsalted butter

GNOCCHI

250g (9 oz)	peeled and diced potato
	knob of butter
1	small egg
60g (2 oz)	flour
25g (1 oz)	grated horseradish
	chopped chives, for garnish

POACHED BEEF FILLET WITH HORSERADISH GNOCCHI

METHOD: Season the meat with salt and pepper. Heat the clarified butter in a large frypan over a high heat, and brown the tournedos well on all sides. Put aside.

SAUCE: Sauté the onions in the same pan over a medium heat until browned. Add the guinness, tomato purée and brown sugar.

Simmer for 2 minutes, then pour into a clean pot. Add the beef stock. Add the bayleaf and thyme, then reduce the liquid to 400–450ml (2 cups), skimming off all impurities as they rise. If desired, at this stage the remaining liquid may be slightly thickened with the arrowroot, diluted in stock. If doing so, continue to simmer for 2 minutes. Put aside until required.

GNOCCHI: Place the potatoes in salted water to cover, and cook over a steady heat until tender. Strain off the water, then return the potatoes to the heat to dry off. While the potatoes are hot, mash or put them through a mouli. Allow to cool.

Beat the butter into the mashed potato, then beat in the egg and finely mix in the sieved flour. Blend in the horseradish. Place the mixture on a floured surface and knead once or twice. Using flour to prevent sticking, carefully roll it out to a thickness of 5mm (¼"). Using a 4cm (1½") cutter, carefully cut out 12 discs, placing them on a floured tray as you go.

Bring a large pot of salted water to the boil. Cook the gnocchi in batches, dropping them into the water and cooking them for 2–3 minutes, or until they float. Drain each batch and place the gnocchi on a lightly buttered plate or baking tray. Once they are all cooked, cover with a piece of buttered greaseproof paper and put aside.

MEAT: Heat the beef stock in an ovenproof dish. Once at a gentle simmer, add the beef. The meat must be covered. Poach to the desired degree; the best results are achieved if the meat is cooked until rare or medium rare. This will take 5–6 minutes.

Once cooked, remove the meat from the stock and drain. Keep covered in a warm place. Remove the string.

TO SERVE: Pass the sauce through a fine sieve into a clean pot. Whisk in a knob of butter and season to taste with pepper and salt. Reheat the gnocchi in a medium oven.

Place each of the tournedos in the centre of a hot dinner plate. Place 2 hot gnocchi on top, overlapping. Coat in plenty of hot guinness sauce, sprinkle with chopped chives and serve immediately, accompanied by Braised Cabbage (see page 130) and glazed root vegetables.

The basic bavarian cream lends itself very well to an endless variety of flavourings both savoury and sweet; liqueurs, fruits, coffee, chocolate . . . the list is endless.

The custard can be made very delicate and light by carefully folding in beaten egg white just before it sets.

KAHLUA BAVAROIS WITH WHITE AND DARK CHOCOLATE SAUCES

BAVAROIS INGREDIENTS
— SERVES 6–8

1 tsp		coffee granules
250ml	(1 cup)	milk
4		egg yolks
60g	(2 oz)	castor sugar
60ml	(4 tbsp)	kahlua
4–5		gelatine leaves or 1 tbsp powdered gelatine
150ml	(⅔ cup)	cream
1		egg white, beaten until fluffy

DARK CHOCOLATE SAUCE

150g	(5 oz)	bitter chocolate couverture
125ml	(½ cup)	milk
2 tbsp	(3 tbsp)	cream

WHITE CHOCOLATE SAUCE

200g	(7 oz)	white chocolate
125ml	(½ cup)	milk
2 tbsp	(3 tbsp)	cream

METHOD: Place the coffee granules in the milk and bring to the boil in a heavy-bottomed pot over medium heat. Whisk the egg yolks with the sugar and kahlua until double in quantity. Pour on a third of the boiled milk and mix together with a wooden spoon.

Pour the egg mixture into the remaining boiled milk. Lower the heat and cook until the custard coats the back of a wooden spoon. Be sure to stir continuously during the cooking process. Remove from the heat.

Soften the gelatine leaves in cold water, squeeze dry, then add to the custard. Stir until completely dissolved. Pass the custard through a fine sieve into a clean stainless steel bowl.

Whip the cream lightly and beat the egg white to a fluffy snow.

Place the custard over a larger bowl of ice and stir until it reaches the thickness of unbeaten egg white. Mix in the whipped cream, then carefully fold in the beaten egg white. Pour into a suitable dish or fill 6 x 100ml (half-cup) moulds. Place in the refrigerator and allow to set for at least 2 hours before serving.

CHOCOLATE SAUCES: Melt the chocolate separately in 2 double saucepans or bains maries.

Bring the milk and cream to the boil in a pot set over a high heat.

Pour the milk and cream into each portion of melted chocolate, stirring continuously.

Pour the chocolate sauces back into the pots, then quickly bring each to the boil for approximately 10 seconds.

Pass each through a fine sieve into a clean stainless steel bowl, cover and allow to cool.

TO SERVE: Release the edges of each bavarois with your finger tips. Briefly dip each mould into warm water. Tip upside down over a small plate and shake out the bavarois. Place each on a chilled plate.

Spoon the chocolate sauces around the bavarois, making a nice design where they meet. Garnish with a few fresh berries and serve.

CHILLED CUCUMBER AND MELON SOUP

Honeydew melons are best for this soup. These are oval melons with a yellow-green skin and delicate green flesh. Telegraph or continental cucumbers, as they are known in Australia, are the cucumbers to use.

METHOD: Scoop out the melon, retaining 100g (4 oz) for garnish. Place the rest in a food processor and liquidise.

Peel the cucumber, cut it in half lengthways, and scoop out the line of seeds. Retain 100g (4 oz) for garnish, and process the remainder as with the melon, then whisk both together.

Crush the mint leaves then add them to the liquid. Cover the mixture firmly and place it in the refrigerator for 5–6 hours, tasting regularly. When the desired mint flavour is reached, remove the mint.

GARNISH: Finely dice the remaining melon and cucumber.
Mix the chives with the sour cream.
Wash the mint.

TO SERVE: Season the chilled soup to taste. Divide the diced melon and cucumber between 6 chilled soup bowls then pour on the soup. Spoon on a dessertspoon of sour cream then garnish with a sprig of mint. Serve chilled.

INGREDIENTS — SERVES 6

1.4 kg (3 lb)	melon
400g (14 oz)	cucumber
8	sprigs mint
	salt and ground pepper
	pinch of sugar (optional)

GARNISH

100g (4 oz)	melon
100g (4 oz)	diced cucumber
2 dsp	finely chopped chives
6 dsp	sour cream
6	sprigs of mint

The base meat used in the preparation of this dish can be anything from pork to pheasant; Huka Lodge savoury farce is very adaptable.

We prefer to use ruby port as a deeper red brown colour is achieved. Madeira may also be used in place of port.

INGREDIENTS — SERVES 6

500g (1 lb)	Basic Noodle Dough using 4 egg yolks (see page 137)
100ml (½ cup)	ruby port
300–400g (12 oz)	Huka Lodge Savoury Farce (see page 136)

SAUCE

40g (2 oz)	shallots, finely diced
100ml (½ cup)	port
50ml (3½ tbsp)	sherry vinegar
100ml (½ cup)	Chicken or White Stock (see page 138)
25ml (2 tbsp)	cream
350g (12 oz)	unsalted butter pepper and salt

GARNISH

1	medium-sized carrot
2	medium-sized courgettes
60g (2 oz)	leek

PORT SCENTED PASTA BAGS

METHOD: Place the port in a small pot and reduce by half over a high heat. Weigh out the pasta ingredients as in the basic recipe, adding the port to the eggs. Prepare as in the basic recipe, (page 137).

Roll out the pasta dough using a pasta roller if you have one or with a rolling pin, using the method as described in the basic recipe. Roll out to a thickness of approximately 1mm.

Cut the pasta sheets into 11cm (4″) wide strips, then at 11cm (4″) intervals across. You will need 18 squares plus a couple for good measure.

Spoon about 20g (2–3 tsps) of savoury farce into the middle of each square. Lightly egg-wash around the edges then bring each corner up to form a bag. Pinch together, separating out the flaps at the top. If you really feel like some work, tie each bag with a thin strip of blanched leek or a piece of chive.

Place the bags on a well-floured tray and rest for 10 minutes before cooking.

TO COOK: Heat plenty of salted water in a large pot. Bring the water to the boil then add 2 tablespoons of cooking oil (olive is best).

Cook the pasta bags in 4 batches; they will take 4–5 minutes to cook. Carefully remove from the water using a slotted spoon, and refresh in cold water. Repeat with the remaining bags. Once all the pasta bags have been cooked and refreshed, place them in a lightly buttered ovenproof dish. Cover with tinfoil and put aside.

SAUCE: Place the shallots, port and vinegar in a pot over medium heat and reduce until almost all evaporated.

Add the chicken stock and reduce by about half. Add the cream and simmer for 1 minute.

Whisk in the butter a knob at a time, rapidly whisking as you go.

Continue until all the butter is incorporated. Season to taste with pepper and salt. Put aside.

GARNISH: Wash and trim the vegetables. Slice the leek in half lengthways then cut into ribbons. Slice the carrot and courgettes lengthways and cut into ribbons.

Blanch each separately in boiling salted water until just crisp. Refresh, drain and put aside until required.

TO SERVE: Heat the pasta bags to serving temperature in a moderate oven. Heat the sauce.

Heat the vegetable garnish in the microwave or by plunging it into boiling water for the count of 5. Drain, then toss in a little hot butter.

Place a bundle of vegetable ribbons in the centre of each plate. Carefully arrange 3 pasta bags around the vegetables, and spoon sauce over each bag. Garnish with fresh herbs and serve while hot.

Dining at Huka Lodge during the warmer months you will be sure to come across a rose petal sorbet or iced soufflé. The beautiful scent and colour of the roses combined with the creamy sweet texture of the sorbet makes a noble end for these proud flowers.

ROSE PETAL AND LEMON SORBET

INGREDIENTS — SERVES 6–8

40g (2 oz)	red rose petals (the ones with the strongest scent have the best flavours)
350ml (1½ cups)	water
100g (4 oz)	sugar
	juice of 2 lemons

METHOD: Very carefully but thoroughly wash the rose petals, then pat them dry between 2 layers of kitchen paper. Retain 6 of the petals for garnish.

Bring the water and sugar to the boil, lower the heat and add the rose petals. Gently simmer for 5 minutes, then allow to cool, leaving the rose petals in the sugar syrup.

Once cool, pass through a fine sieve into a clean bowl, add the lemon juice and mix together. Finely dice the retained petals and mix them into the liquid.

Place in a sorbetière and freeze, or place in a bowl in the freezer, whisking regularly during freezing.

TO SERVE: Pipe or spoon into elegant chilled glasses, garnish with a little lemon zest and serve immediately.

ROAST POUSSIN
WITH ROSEMARY BUTTER

METHOD: Prepare the poussin for roasting, using whichever method you prefer. Spread clarified butter over each poussin, then sprinkle with salt and ground pepper. Wrap 2 bacon rashers around the breast part of each poussin.

Preheat the oven to 220°C (430°F). Place the poussins in a roasting tray, pour over the honey then roast, basting regularly, for 10 minutes. Remove the bacon, lower the temperature to 180°C (350°F) and continue to roast and baste for a further 5 minutes.

Remove the poussins from the oven, place on a clean tray and put aside in a warm place until required.

ROSEMARY BUTTER: Place the crushed garlic and the butter in a small sauté pan over a high heat until the butter begins to froth. Add the rosemary and continue cooking until a light brown colour is reached. Add the lemon juice then remove from the heat. Season with salt and ground pepper.

TO SERVE: Place a roasted poussin on each hot dinner plate, and evenly spoon over the nut brown rosemary butter. If desired, a cordon of gravy or jus may be dropped around the poussin at this stage.

Garnish with a sprig of fresh rosemary. Serve with a rice timbale and simply prepared seasonal vegetables.

Poussin or spatchcock are small, immature chickens which are generally served spit-cooked in a hot oven or over a grill. One poussin is served per portion.

As with all small birds which are served whole, there is a dilemma of whether to bone them out or leave them whole with the bones in. Another alternative is to roast them whole then remove the breast and thigh, etc., when serving, which can be somewhat difficult.

We prefer to split the poussin down the backbone and remove the rib cage, backbone and thighbone, leaving only the drumstick in.

This dish is another good chance to use a savoury farce filling. Once the poussin has been boned out, a quantity of chicken-based savoury farce may be placed inside. The poussin is then moulded back to its original shape, tied and roasted in a slightly cooler oven. In both cases basting is essential. Fresh chicken is best; though frozen chickens are still generally of good quality and cheaper.

INGREDIENTS — SERVES 6

6	cleaned poussin (spatchcock)
	clarified butter
	pepper and salt
12	bacon rashers
3 tbsp (4 tbsp)	clear honey
1	clove garlic, crushed
150g (5 oz)	unsalted butter
	fresh rosemary
1 tbsp	lemon juice

GARNISH

	fresh rosemary sprigs
	a little gravy
	(optional)

Use Golden Delicious or other dessert apples in this tarte.

The base is made from puff pastry and must be rolled out very thinly to stop it from rising too high, yet ensure it is light.

If calvados is unavailable, brandy or even apple juice may be used instead. As an alternative to the sabayon, almond marzipan paste may be placed under the apple, rolled out slightly smaller than the pastry base.

APPLE TARTES

INGREDIENTS — SERVES 6

6	medium-sized dessert apples, peeled, cored and halved (keep in a little lemon water to prevent browning)
400g (14 oz)	Puff Pastry (see page 144) (6 rounds) 14cm (6″) in diameter
30g (1 oz)	castor sugar
6 tsp-sized	knobs of butter a little Sugar Syrup (see page 146)

SABAYON

5	egg yolks
100g (4 oz)	sugar
60ml (4 tbsp)	calvados

METHOD: Slice the apples very thinly. Using a fork prick each pastry base all over to prevent it rising.

Arrange the apple in circles on the pastry bases, each circle facing the opposite way to the previous one. Sprinkle each with castor sugar then dot all over with butter.

Preheat the oven to 170°C (350°F) then bake the tartes on a baking sheet for approximately 15 minutes. Make sure the pastry is cooked and the apples have turned a light brown.

To enhance the colour further if necessary, remove the tartes from the oven once cooked, place them under the grill or salamander and caramelise, being careful not to burn.

SABAYON: Place all the ingredients in a sabayon basin or round-bottomed bowl over a pot of simmering water. Using a balloon whisk beat the mixture until the sugar has dissolved and the sabayon is pale yellow and double in quantity. Do this just before serving.

TO SERVE: Glaze each tarte with a little sugar syrup. Using a plate with a rim, pour on the sabayon. Place the warm apple tarte over the sabayon and garnish with a sprig of fresh mint. Serve immediately.

CHILLED AVOCADO SOUP

Top quality ripe avocados in prime condition must be used for this soup. It must also be made close to serving time as it does not keep.

METHOD: Cut the avocados in half and remove the stones, using the heel of a large knife. Peel the avocados, working back from the pointed end.

Retain half an avocado for garnish. Cover in plastic wrap to avoid discolouring. Place the remaining avocado in a food processor and process until smooth. Add the lemon juice and chicken stock.

Pass into a clean bowl. Add the cream and season to taste with salt and white pepper.

Dice the half-avocado into small cubes.

TO SERVE: Divide the soup evenly between 6 chilled bowls. Sprinkle in the diced avocado, spoon on the yoghurt, then sprinkle over chopped parsley and paprika. Serve immediately.

INGREDIENTS — SERVES 6

3		avocados
50ml	(3½ tbsp)	lemon juice
800ml	(3½ cups)	Chicken Stock (see page 138)
100ml	(½ cup)	cream
		seasoning

GARNISH

6 dsp	plain, unsweetened yoghurt
	chopped parsley
	pinch paprika

Hoki is a deepwater fish found around New Zealand and south-eastern Australia. It may be processed into large boneless fillets which have a delicate flavour. Once cooked, hoki must be handled very carefully as it flakes very easily.

White muscat grapes are best for this dish; they are large and have a rich, full flavour.

BAKED HOKI

INGREDIENTS — SERVES 6

600g	(1¼ lb)	trimmed hoki loin
50g	(2 oz)	walnuts, very finely chopped
50g	(2 oz)	hazelnuts, very finely chopped
100g	(4 oz)	almonds, very finely chopped
100g	(4 oz)	brioche or white breadcrumbs
		seasoned flour for coating
		clarified butter, melted
		ground pepper and salt

BEURRE BLANC

3		small shallots
100ml	(½ cup)	dry champagne or méthode champenoise
50ml	(3½ tbsp)	champagne or white wine vinegar
100ml	(½ cup)	Fish Stock (see page 139)
50ml	(3½ tbsp)	cream
350g	(12 oz)	unsalted butter, cut into small pieces
		seasoning
21		muscat grapes

METHOD: Mix the chopped nuts and breadcrumbs together. Lightly coat the hoki pieces in seasoned flour, shake off the excess, then dip in clarified butter.

Press one side of the fillets into the nut mixture. Pat down, then place the fish in an oven dish, nut side up. Season and put aside until ready for baking.

SAUCE: Place the shallots, champagne and champagne vinegar in a heavy-bottomed pot over a high heat, and reduce until almost all evaporated.

Add the fish stock and simmer for 2 minutes; add the cream and simmer for 1 minute.

Lower the heat, then rapidly whisk in the butter a piece at a time until it is all incorporated.

Season to taste and remove from the heat.

Plunge the whole grapes into boiling water for the count of 5. Remove and plunge into iced water. Peel, cut in half and seed the grapes. Put aside until required.

COOKING THE FISH: Preheat the oven to 190°C (375°F) and bake the hoki for 7–8 minutes. Remove the fish from the oven then brown the nut crust lightly under a grill or salamander.

TO SERVE: Using a fish slice, very carefully remove each piece of hoki from the baking dish. Dab onto a piece of kitchen paper to remove any excess butter. Place on a hot plate, and arrange 7 pieces of grape around each piece of fish.

Evenly spoon the beurre blanc around the hoki. Garnish with a sprig of fennel and serve while hot.

LEMON AND PERRIER SORBET

INGREDIENTS — SERVES 6

2	285ml bottles Perrier water
50g (2 oz)	sugar
	lemon juice of 3 medium-sized lemons

This refreshing, tangy sorbet can be quite icy, as the sugar content is low. It is therefore often easier to spoon rather than pipe it into the glass.

METHOD: Add the sugar to the Perrier water over a gentle heat, stirring until the sugar has dissolved.

Allow to cool then add the lemon juice. Pass into a clean bowl and freeze, or process in a sorbetière. Serve in chilled tall glasses.

WILD BOAR CUTLETS

Generally only the legs and saddle of wild boar are used, and they are usually well marinated or well hung beforehand.

The procedure and marinade are the same as for venison, rabbit or hare, although the timing will vary. Use a cooked marinade (see rabbit and hare recipes pages 50, 81) and marinate for at least 24 hours and up to 48 hours.

Younger boar up to one year old is the most tasty. Some say the head is the best part, stuffed and served cold . . . I'll stick to the legs and saddle! Boar may be bought commercially from some butchers or game suppliers.

INGREDIENTS — SERVES 6

12	boar cutlets, about 85g (3 oz) each salt and ground pepper clarified butter

CUMBERLAND SAUCE

100ml (½ cup)	redcurrant jelly
1	shallot, finely diced
2 tbsp (3 tbsp)	port
	juice of 1 orange
	juice of ½ lemon
	zest of ½ orange, julienned

METHOD: Make the sauce first. Melt the jelly. Blanch the diced shallot in a little boiling water then drain and add to the jelly. Add the port and juices, and bring to the boil. Add the zest and lower the heat. Gently cook for 1 minute. Cover and keep just warm until required.

BOAR CUTLETS: Season each cutlet with salt and ground pepper. Heat the clarified butter in a large sauté pan. Sauté the cutlets in batches until medium-cooked. Keep warm.

TO SERVE: Place 2 boar cutlets on each plate, and spoon on the cumberland sauce. Garnish with fresh watercress and serve with turnip purée and carrots.

The kiwifruit used in this dessert should be ripe but firm. Be absolutely sure the oil in which you deepfry the fruit is fresh and very clean. The kiwifruit may also be shallow-fried in a little very hot clarified butter.

KIWIFRUIT IN CINNAMON BATTER

INGREDIENTS – SERVES 6

6	medium-sized kiwifruit
	oil or clarified butter for frying
	flour
	castor sugar

BATTER

1	egg
1 tsp	sugar
½ tsp	cinnamon
250ml (1 cup)	milk
125g (4 oz)	flour

CHOCOLATE SAUCE

200g (7 oz)	chocolate (bitter couverture)
25g (1 oz)	sugar
175ml (¾ cup)	cream
	cream for garnish
6	sprigs mint

METHOD: Using a small, sharp knife, top and tail each kiwifruit then stand it on end and cut off the skin in strips. Cut each kiwifruit in half lengthways then into quarters.

BATTER: Beat the egg, mix in the sugar and cinnamon, then the milk.

Sprinkle on the flour, mixing vigorously as you go until a coating consistency is achieved. Pass through a fine sieve into a clean bowl.

CHOCOLATE SAUCE: Melt the chocolate in a double saucepan or bain marie.

Add the sugar to the cream, then heat over medium heat to just below boiling point, stirring regularly. Pour the cream into the melted chocolate, stirring as you go. Once well mixed, pass into a clean container ready for use.

A knob of butter may be whisked in at this stage to enhance the flavour and shine. Cover a piece of greaseproof paper to prevent a skin from forming. Do not refrigerate.

COOKING KIWIFRUIT AND SERVING: Heat the oil or butter to a slight blue haze (not smoke) – 350–380°C (175–195°F). Lightly coat each piece of kiwifruit in plain flour. In batches of 4, dip the kiwifruit in the batter. Allow the excess batter to drain off. Carefully drop 4 pieces of kiwifruit at a time into the hot fat or oil, making sure they don't stick together.

Cook until golden brown all over, remove from the oil onto a piece of kitchen paper, then toss in castor sugar. Place on a tray in a warm place.

Repeat this process with the remaining kiwifruit, allowing the oil to recover heat after each batch.

Flood 6 plates, at room temperature, with chocolate sauce. Arrange 4 pieces of deep-fried kiwifruit on each plate.

Dribble a cordon of cream around and feather with a small knife. Garnish with a sprig of mint and serve warm.

SALMON SALAD

INGREDIENTS — SERVES 6

approx. 350g	(12 oz)	raw salmon, trimmed and boned

POACHING STOCK

1kg	(2 lb)	salmon bones and trimmings
500ml	(2½ cups)	dry white wine
500ml	(2½ cups)	water
1		bayleaf
25g	(1 oz)	chopped carrot
1		medium-sized onion, roughly chopped
25g	(1 oz)	leek
1		stalk of parsley
4		white peppercorns
		a little salt

MAYONNAISE

3–4		egg yolks
½ tsp		mustard
1 tsp		white wine vinegar
		juice of 1 lemon
100ml	(½ cup)	grapeseed or sunflower oil (at room temperature)
150ml	(⅔ cup)	salad oil (at room temperature)
1 tsp		chives
1		small shallot
25ml	(2 tbsp)	sherry vinegar
25ml	(2 tbsp)	cream
		pepper and salt

SALAD

30		small leaves butterhead lettuce
30g	(1 oz)	button mushrooms, sliced
60g	(2 oz)	fennel bulb, sliced
		ground pepper and salt
6		sprigs of fennel

POACHING STOCK: Roughly chop the bones, etc. Place them in a large pot and add the wine and water. Bring to the boil over a gentle heat, skimming off all impurities as they rise. Add the vegetables and herbs, and simmer for 20–30 minutes. Pass through a fine sieve into a clean container. Allow to cool.

MAYONNAISE: Place the egg yolks, mustard, vinegar and lemon juice together in a bowl or mixing machine and whisk to the ribbon stage. It should double in quantity and turn a pale yellow colour. Make sure the oil is at room temperature. Pour in the oil very slowly, whisking continuously until it is all incorporated. Season to taste with pepper and salt.

Finely chop the chives and very finely dice the shallot. Add the sherry vinegar, shallot and chives to the mayonnaise.

Correct the consistency with cream if necessary. Cover and put aside, out of the refrigerator, until required.

SALAD: Wash and pat dry the lettuce leaves.
Wash and thinly slice the mushrooms.
Trim away the stalks of the fennel bulb and string it as you would celery. Cut it in half then slice across thinly.

POACHING FISH: Cover the salmon in the cool or cold stock and bring to a simmer over medium heat. Poach the fish until just underdone, i.e. still a darker shade of pink inside.

Remove from the stock, drain and allow to cool completely. If possible poach the fish the day before and allow it to set in the refrigerator overnight, firmly covered.

CONSTRUCTION AND SERVING: Very carefully flake the salmon then lightly mix it with the mushroom and fennel. Place in a clean bowl then mix in the mayonnaise, trying not to break the salmon up too much.

Arrange the lettuce leaves on cool plates, and spoon on the salmon salad. Garnish with sprigs of fennel and serve.

Although Californian quail are plentiful in New Zealand in the wild, practically all quail found in commercial kitchens come from quail farms. Their quality is consistent and they may be purchased fresh or frozen.

Usually they require no hanging or cleaning; if you are a true game lover you may decide to age the birds further to enhance the flavour. At no time should the quail smell bad or off.

As with other birds roasted whole there is the dilemma of whether to bone them out or not. There is no doubt that quail are difficult to eat if the bones are left in. They are already small, so we recommend removing most of the main bones using a small vegetable knife. Usually we leave only the drumstick in. This is a fiddly job but worth the time. Sometimes, once the rib cage has been removed, we fill the quail with a tasty farce; in this case we would only serve 1 bird for an entree; without stuffing 2 birds are necessary.

INGREDIENTS — SERVES 6

12		quail
		ground pepper and salt
12		rashers bacon
		clarified butter
		a little honey (optional)
150ml	(⅔ cup)	madeira
200ml	(1 cup)	Brown Game Stock (see page 140)
25g	(1 oz)	butter
12		Brioche Croûtons (see page 143)

ROAST QUAIL

METHOD: Split the quail down the backbone, open out and press down flat on a cutting board, breast side down. Using a small vegetable knife remove the rib cage, breast bone, wing bones and thigh bones, leaving only the drumstick intact. Try to keep the quail intact during the boning. Repeat this process with all the quail. Retain the bones.

Season the quail on both sides with pepper and salt. Tuck all loose flaps under the breast and tie the legs so that they cross over at the end. Wrap each in bacon.

Preheat the oven to 180–200° C (350–400° F). Brush the quail with clarified butter and honey, and place in a roasting tray. Roast for 15 minutes, or until only just pink. Once cooked, remove the quail from the heat, cover, and place in a warm place.

Place the quail bones in the roasting pan and brown well over a medium heat. Drain off the excess fat or butter. Add the madeira, simmer for 2 minutes, then add the stock. Lower the heat and simmer for a further 2–4 minutes, then pass through a fine sieve into a clean pot. Bring to the boil, skim, then season to taste.

TO SERVE: Cut out 12 brioche croûtons 5–10mm (¼–½″) thick with a 4cm (2″) round cutter. Lightly fry or toast on both sides.

Heat the jus to serving temperature, and whisk in 25g (1 oz) butter.

Place 2 croûtons on each hot plate. Remove the bacon from the quail then place a quail on each croûton. Evenly spoon over the jus.

Garnish with fresh thyme and caramelised orange segments.

MINT SORBET

METHOD: Bring the water and sugar to the boil. Roughly chop 5 of the mint leaves and add them to the sugar syrup. Lower the heat and simmer gently for 5 minutes. Remove from the heat and allow to cool. Place in a liquidiser and process until well infused.

Pass through a medium sieve into a clean bowl, and mix in the lemon juice. Chop 5 mint sprigs and add. Place in a freezerproof bowl or a sorbetière and freeze.

Serve chilled, garnished with a sprig of mint.

INGREDIENTS — SERVES 6

300ml	(1¼ cups)	water
90g	(3 oz)	sugar
16		sprigs of mint
		juice of one lemon

Be careful not to overcook veal, as it is usually very lean and will become dry if overcooked or cooked in insufficient clarified butter or oil. Escalopes are usually cut from the filled end of the leg or from the cushion or nut, and can be bought ready-cut. Veal has an unassertive flavour and adapts well to other strong savoury flavours.

VEAL ESCALOPES

INGREDIENTS — SERVES 6

6	veal escalopes, approx. 75g (3 oz) each
	salt and ground pepper
2–3	
tsp	clarified butter

SAUCE

1 tsp	butter
1	medium-sized shallot, finely diced
½	clove garlic, crushed
60g (2 oz)	button mushrooms, sliced thinly
300ml (1¼ cups)	Demi-Glaze (see page 141)
125g (4 oz)	tomato, diced and blanched
	salt and pepper
½ tsp	chopped basil
½ tsp	chopped parsley
½ tsp	chopped tarragon
	julienne of pimento, for garnish

METHOD: Trim the veal escalopes if necessary, removing any sinew etc. Flatten out between layers of plastic wrap and lightly pound with a meat hammer.

SAUCE: Melt the butter in a small sauté pan. Add the shallots and crushed garlic and cook gently for 3 minutes. Add the sliced mushrooms and cook for 2 minutes.

Add the demi-glaze, simmer for 5 minutes, then add the tomato and continue to simmer for 3-5 minutes. Season to taste, remove from the heat and put aside until required.

COOKING ESCALOPES AND SERVING: Season the prepared escalopes on both sides. Heat the clarified butter in a large sauté pan over a high heat. Quickly sauté the escalopes, a couple of minutes each side, allowing the sauté pan to recover its heat before you add further escalopes. Keep the escalopes warm.

Heat the sauce to serving temperature and add the chopped herbs.

Divide the sauce between 6 hot dinner plates. Cut each escalope into 3 and arrange over the sauce. Garnish each with a small bundle of blanched pimento julienne. Serve immediately, accompanied by saffron rice and crisp vegetables.

CRÈME BRÛLÉE

Crème brûlée is a classical dessert, rich and sweet and very easy to prepare. There are many variation possible with crème brûlée; adding fruits and berries to flavour the custard, or liqueurs and spices, all result in a wonderfully enjoyable end to any meal.

METHOD: Place the vanilla pod in the cream. Place over high heat and bring almost to the boil, but do not allow to boil.

Meanwhile beat the egg yolks and sugar together until they have become light yellow and doubled in quantity. Pour on the scalded cream, mixing as you go. Remove the vanilla pod.

Place over a double saucepan or bain marie and continue to cook, stirring continuously, until the custard coats the back of a wooden spoon. The custard must be quite thick.

Pour into 6 ovenproof ramekins, place in the refrigerator and allow to cool completely and set.

TO SERVE: Heat the grill or salamander to high. Spread an even layer of brown sugar approximately 3mm (¹/₈″) thick, over the top of each cream. With a damp cloth clean off any drips of sugar crystal from the sides and rim of the ramekins.

In batches of 2–3 caramelise the sugar under the grill; try to achieve quite a dark colour. Serve the crème brûlée while the sugar is still warm.

NOTE: Vanilla pods may be used several times. Put them to maximum use by filling a suitable container with sugar and storing the vanilla pods in the sugar. The flavour and aroma of the pods will be absorbed by the sugar and you will have vanilla sugar; very useful in baking and dessert preparation. Top it up as you use it.

INGREDIENTS — SERVES 6

250ml	(1 cup)	cream
1		vanilla pod
8		egg yolks
50g	(2 oz)	castor sugar
		brown sugar

RABBIT AND VEGETABLE BROTH

The success of a broth depends on the quality of the base stock. Try to keep it as clear as possible and if necessary reduce the quantity to increase the flavour.

Traditionally a broth is thickened with barley as no flour or roux is used. We prefer to omit the barley as well, so the result is a highly flavoured stock garnished with diced vegetables and meat.

INGREDIENTS — SERVES 6

2 litres	(3½ pints)	white rabbit stock (see Chicken Stock) page 138)
50g	(2 oz)	carrot, turnip, leek, celery and onion
1		small bayleaf
1		stalk of parsley
1		sprig of thyme
25g	(1 oz)	clarified butter
150–200g	(5–7 oz)	rabbit meat from saddle or thigh
		pepper and salt
1 tbsp		chopped parsley

METHOD: Pour the stock into a large pot and place over a medium heat. Gently simmer until it has reduced to 1500ml (2½ pints).

Peel and wash the vegetables and cut them in 2mm (¹/₈″) dice. Add to the reduced stock, along with the herbs. Cook for the further 20–30 minutes, or until the vegetables are tender.

Heat the clarified butter in a large sauté pan. Brown the rabbit meat on both sides then roast in a medium oven. Remove from the oven and drain on kitchen paper. Allow to cool, then dice the meat into tidy cubes.

After 30 minutes remove the parsley stalk, bayleaf and thyme from the broth. Season to taste with pepper and salt.

TO SERVE: Heat the broth to serving temperature. Check the seasoning, and add the chopped parsley and diced meat. Pour into hot soup bowls and serve while hot.

SCALLOPS ON BLINIS

Scallops are available all year round and are very versatile. Great care must be taken not to overcook them, however, as they shrink and become tough.

A blini is made from a yeast batter and resembles a pikelet. The batter should be used within an hour of making or it will ferment further and the flavour will spoil. You will, however, need to ferment the basic yeast and milk mixture for 1½ hours.

BLINI BATTER: Warm the milk to blood temperature then dissolve the fresh yeast in it. Mix in about 20g (1oz) of the flour. Cover and allow to ferment at room temperature for one and a half hours.

Once ready, mix in the remaining flour and the egg yolk. Rest for 15 minutes, then season.

Whisk the egg white until stiff, then carefully fold it into the batter.

Melt half the clarified butter in a large pan. Place 3 tablespoons of batter at a time in the pan, making sure they don't run into each other. (You will need a total of 18.) Cook for 40 seconds each side, then drain on kitchen paper. When halfway through, wipe out the frypan and melt the remaining clarified butter, then continue as before. Cover and keep at room temperature.

SAUCE: Place the shallots, wine and vinegar in a pot, and reduce over high heat until almost all evaporated.

Add the fish stock, tomato paste and basil, and reduce by half. Add the cream and lower the heat. Simmer gently until the sauce just begins to thicken. Remove from the heat and put aside until required.

Blanch the tomatoes by plunging them into boiling water for the count of 5 then putting them straight into iced water. Remove the skins, quarter and remove all seeds. Dice the flesh into small cubes and put aside until required.

SCALLOPS: Clean and trim the scallops, and remove the roes. Retain 12 roes. Heat the clarified butter in a large sauté pan. Season the scallops with pepper and salt, and cook in batches for 10–15 seconds each side. Drain on kitchen paper and keep warm. Sauté the roe for 4 seconds each side.

TO SERVE: Pass the sauce into a clean pot; season to taste. Whisk in a knob of butter. Heat to serving temperature.

Place 3 blinis on each hot plate; divide the scallops between the plates.

Add the diced tomato to the sauce, then spoon the sauce around the scallops and blini. Garnish with a sprig of fresh basil.

INGREDIENTS – SERVES 6

6-9	scallops per portion, depending on size
	clarified butter
	salt and pepper

BLINI BATTER

125ml	(½ cup)	milk
7g	(¼ oz)	fresh yeast
75g	(3 oz)	flour
1		egg yolk
1		egg white
		seasoning
50g	(2 oz)	clarified butter

SAUCE

2		shallots, finely diced
200ml	(1 cup)	white wine
50ml	(3½ tbsp)	champagne or white wine vinegar
800ml	(3½ cups)	Fish Stock (see page 139)
3 tbsp	(4 tbsp)	tomato paste
1 tbsp		fresh basil
400ml	(1¾ cups)	cream
2		tomatoes, blanched and diced
		pepper and salt
15g	(½ oz)	unsalted butter
6		basil leaves

MUSCAT GRAPE SORBET

Green or black muscats may be used in this sorbet. Ripe muscats are large and richly perfumed, perfect for a sorbet. Remove all seeds before processing the grapes as they may have a bitter taste.

INGREDIENTS — SERVES 6

100ml	(½ cup)	water
50g	(2 oz)	sugar
400g	(14 oz)	ripe muscat grapes
		juice of 1 lemon
6		whole grapes for garnish

METHOD: Bring the water and sugar to the boil. Cool. Cut the grapes in half and remove the seeds.

Add the lemon juice to the syrup. Liquidise the grapes, then pass them through a fine sieve. Mix with the sugar syrup.

Place in a sorbet machine or freeze in a large bowl, whisking regularly to achieve a smooth texture.

TO SERVE: Cut the garnishing grapes in half, remove the seeds, then cut them into quarters. Pipe the sorbet into chilled glasses then sprinkle over the quartered grapes. Serve immediately.

PIGEON WITH BRAISED CABBAGE

Pigeon is available in New Zealand from specialist game outlets. Usually 4–5-week-old birds, called squabs, are sold; these have quite a pleasant gamy flavour.

They can be tough, so some ageing may be needed; they may also be marinated. We only use the breast meat for serving and make the sauce from the remaining carcass and legs. The result is a beautiful full, rich jus or sauce.

GARNISH: Wash and dry the mushrooms. If using dried cèpes and chanterelles, soak them in warm water for 30 minutes. Drain and dry.

Heat the butter in a sauté pan and cook the mushrooms until quite well done. Drain on kitchen paper and put aside ready for use.

PIGEON: Remove the breast from each pigeon, leaving the skin on. Trim the wing bone back to the first joint and clean the remaining bone. Chop the remaining carcasses into 4 and put aside for the sauce.

Heat the walnut oil in a sauté pan and brown the pigeon breasts on all sides. Put aside.

SAUCE: Heat a roasting tray on the stove top and add a little oil. Add the chopped pigeon bones and brown lightly on all sides. Add the prepared vegetables and mix together. Place in a medium oven and roast until well browned.

Return to the stove top and place over medium heat. Add the vinegar, madeira and redcurrant jelly, and mix in well. Bring to the boil then lower the heat and simmer gently for 2 minutes. Add the mushroom trimmings, and the bayleaf. Quickly roast the juniper berries then add to the bones. Add the game stock.

Increase the heat and bring to the boil. Skim. Pour the contents of the roasting tray into a pot and reduce by half over gentle heat. Pass through a fine sieve into a clean pot and reduce down to 200ml (1 cup). Put aside ready for the next step.

CABBAGE AND PIGEON: Remove the stalks from the cabbage then slice thinly. Melt the clarified butter in a casserole and add the cabbage. Cook for 2 minutes. Season with pepper and salt then add the chicken stock, herbs and vinegar. Cover and cook for 5 minutes on the stove top.

Place the browned pigeon breast on the cabbage, replace the casserole lid and cook in a preheated oven at 170°C (325°F) for 30 minutes.

TO SERVE: Bring the sauce to the boil. If you wish, at this stage you may thicken the sauce with arrowroot diluted in a little madeira; if doing so, simmer for 2 minutes once the arrowroot has been whisked in. Check the seasoning then whisk in the knob of butter. Pass through a fine sieve into a clean pot. Add the mushrooms.

Remove the pigeon from the casserole. Divide the cabbage between 6 hot plates. Place the pigeon breast on top. Spoon over the mushroom sauce, garnish with fresh herbs and serve with Parsley Potatoes (see page 135) and Braised Shallots (see page 129).

INGREDIENTS — SERVES 6

12		breasts from 6 x 250–300g (about 10 oz) pigeons
25ml	(2 tbsp)	walnut oil
200g	(7 oz)	raw red cabbage
25g	(1 oz)	clarified butter
		ground pepper and salt
75ml	(⅓ cup)	Chicken Stock (see page 138)
½ tsp		dried mixed herbs
½ tbsp		red wine vinegar

SAUCE

		remaining bones from pigeon carcasses, roughly chopped
1		medium-sized carrot, sliced
1		small onion, sliced
50g	(2 oz)	celery, roughly chopped
2 tbsp	(3 tbsp)	sherry vinegar
50ml	(3½ tbsp)	madeira
1 tbsp		redcurrant jelly
50g	(2 oz)	mixed mushroom trimmings (cèpes, chanterelles, buttons)
1		bayleaf
4		juniper berries
800ml	(3½ cups)	Brown Game Stock (see page 140)
2g	(1 tsp)	arrowroot (optional)
		pepper and salt
		knob of butter

GARNISH

24		small button mushrooms
15g	(½ oz)	diced cèpes (optional)
		small chanterelles (optional)
25g	(1 oz)	clarified butter

PEARS WITH CHOCOLATE GANACHE AND PRALINE

METHOD: Place all the poaching ingredients in a medium-sized pot. Bring to the boil, then lower to a simmer.

Add the prepared pears and poach over medium heat until they are soft; 25–30 minutes. Do not overcook or the pears will not hold their shape; remove the pears from the heat and allow them to cool in the poaching liquid overnight, covering the pot with plastic wrap. Make sure the pot is non-reactive to acids.

The next day remove the pears from the liquid and drain on a clean cloth. Cut off the top, creating a lid. Holding the pear the right way up, scoop out the core and pips with a melon baller, making a cavity for the ganache. Put the pears aside until required for the next step.

Return the poaching syrup to a medium-high heat and reduce to approximately 240ml (1 cup). Cool at room temperature.

CHOCOLATE GANACHE: Chop the chocolate then melt it in a bowl over a pot of simmering water.

Bring the cream to the boil then add it to the chocolate. Mix together thoroughly. Remove from the heat and allow to cool at room temperature, stirring regularly until a piping consistency is reached.

Using a medium-sized star nozzle and piping bag, carefully fill each pear then replace the lid. Cover and place in the refrigerator until required.

PRALINE: Roughly chop the lightly browned almonds. Place the sugar in a pot and melt over a medium to high heat until a pale brown caramel is reached. Stir in the almonds.

Remove from the heat and pour the praline onto a lightly greased baking sheet, spreading or rolling it out until it is approximately 1cm (½″) thick. Allow to cool and harden.

Once cold, crush the praline into quite a fine coating, using a meat hammer or rolling pin. Cover the praline with a clean cloth to prevent it from going everywhere during crushing.

SERVING: Remove the pears from the refrigerator half an hour before serving. Lightly coat each pear with praline, pressing it against the pear firmly with your hand.

Place each pear carefully in the centre of a chilled plate, taking care not to drop praline all over the plate.

Evenly spoon the cooled and reduced poaching liquid around each pear. Garnish with a mint leaf and serve.

We usually use Winter Coles for this dish; as with the Pears Poached in Grenadine (see page 40) choose medium-sized, firm pears which are totally unblemished.

Pears and chocolate are another one of those superb flavour combinations that seem to be made for each other. Poach the pears the day before, allowing plenty of cooling time.

INGREDIENTS — SERVES 6

6	firm pears, peeled and left whole, with the stalk left on
200g (7oz)	sugar
	juice of 1 lemon
600–800ml (about 3 cups)	water, to just cover pears
½	cinnamon stick
½	small bayleaf
100ml (½ cup)	Williams eau de vie

CHOCOLATE GANACHE

200g (7 oz)	dark chocolate
100ml (½ cup)	cream

PRALINE

125g (4oz)	almonds, lightly browned in a hot oven
150g (5oz)	castor sugar

BATTERIE DE CUISINE

1. Heavy duty chopping board
2. Chef's knife in wooden stand
3. Double-bladed knife
4. Fine sieve
5. Canvas piping bag
6. Copper sabayon basin
7. Copper icing sugar shaker
8. General purpose whisk
9. Fancy oval dariole mould

10. Medium copper pot
11. Barquette mould
12. Fine sauce sieve
13. Cane whisk
14. Jelly mould
15. Funnel
16. Ladles
17. Fancy mould
18. Fluted pastry cutter

19. Small terrines
20. Brioche mould
21. Tartlet mould
22. Dariole mould
23. Piping nozzles
24. Savarin mould
25. Wooden rolling pin
26. Ovenware terrine
27. Hair sieve for passing fish mousses
28. Specialised wooden spoons

VEGETABLES

Using only good quality fresh produce is essential for the success of most vegetable dishes, whether they are exotic or not. When purchasing any vegetables, take time to look for basic quality points so you can tell whether the product is wholesome, fresh and in the best possible condition.

All natural colours should be distinctive and you should look for blemishes, bruising, spade and knife marks and, of course, bad patches. Any stalks or foliage left on the vegetable should be fresh looking and upright, not wilted and dull. Any dirt on the vegetables, and there shouldn't be too much, must look fresh and not powdery or dusty, and look for bug tracks or droppings.

Ensure the vegetables are handled and packed properly, and at no time settle for anything less than what you want.

Finally, get to know your local vegetable suppliers. They may have a wealth of knowledge which will be of value to you. Let them know what you like to see in the produce you buy and what in particular you require.

Once you've bought your vegetables and you're ready to use them, treat them with the respect they deserve. Vegetables aren't just accompaniments to the main item, they are as important as anything else in serving a successful dish.

Try to find a happy medium with regard to the degree to which you cook vegetables such as carrots, turnips, etc. They should be cooked through, but you may prefer some crispness. Green beans, snow peas, asparagus and other green vegetables should be crisp, or 'al dente'.

Most baby vegetables — carrots, beans, asparagus, broccoli, cauliflower, snow and sugar peas — can be blanced prior to serving. Once cleaned and trimmed they are placed in plenty of boiling salted water and cooked until just underdone, then removed from the boiling water and plunged straight into iced water.

This will immediately halt the cooking process, preventing the often delicate vegetables from overcooking, and further enhance their natural colours. Blanching also kills the enzymes that break down food, causing it to go bad. Therefore, once blanched and covered, vegetables will keep longer, if required.

Finally, flavourings and sauces should enhance vegetables, not overpower them.

This chapter covers our favourite vegetable dishes and preparations relevant to the menus in this book.

In recent years a much wider variety of fresh vegetables has become available in New Zealand. Not so long ago baby vegetables were unheard of, now everything from baby carrots to baby cauliflower is available. However, beautiful vegetable dishes can also be prepared from traditional, inexpensive products such as carrots, cabbage and potatoes, plus many more.

More often than not, we find that when we have a wonderful variety of fresh vegetables in excellent condition the most satisfying way to prepare them is the simplest.

RATATOUILLE

Ratatouille is a great classic vegetable dish. A perfect accompaniment for lamb, or wonderful on its own.

Ratatouille can be made a day ahead and reheated. Like many dishes flavoured with fresh herbs, it often tastes better the next day.

Some classic restaurants serve ratatouille cold as an hors d'oeuvre; personally I prefer it hot. There are, however, many ways to serve ratatouille and many accompaniments to serve with it.

METHOD: Heat one-third of the olive oil in a sauté pan. Sauté the diced onion until tender then add the garlic. Continue to sauté for 2 minutes; don't allow to colour. Add the diced tomato and the tomato paste and cook for 2 minutes. Add all the herbs except the chopped parsley and mix in. Remove the onion and tomato from the pan. Wipe the pan out a little then add another third of the olive oil. Add the red and green peppers and cook until tender; remove from the pan. Add the remaining oil and sauté the eggplant and courgette. Cook over quite a high heat until they begin to colour.

Mix all the ingredients together in an ovenproof casserole dish, season to taste with salt and ground pepper. Don't over-stir. Cover the casserole and cook in a preheated oven at 200°C (400°F) for 10–15 minutes.

TO SERVE: Remove the ratatouille from the oven, carefully mix in the chopped parsley, check the seasoning. Serve as required.

INGREDIENTS – SERVES 6

100ml (½ cup)	virgin olive oil
1	medium-sized onion, finely diced
4	cloves garlic, crushed
500g (1 lb)	ripe tomato, blanched, seeded and diced
1 dsp	tomato paste
1	bayleaf
2	sprigs rosemary
1	sprig thyme
1	small red pepper, diced
1	small green pepper, diced
300g (10 oz)	eggplant, cut into 5mm (¹/₅″) cubes
400g (14 oz)	courgette, finely diced
1 dsp	chopped parsley

SAUTÉED EGGPLANT

METHOD: The eggplant should be sautéed just before serving, as follows. Sauté in batches to maintain the heat in the pan.

Heat some of the olive oil in a large sauté pan. Rub each slice of eggplant with garlic on both sides. Season with salt and ground pepper, then quickly sauté until golden on each side.

Place on a dish lined with paper to drain off excess oil, and keep warm. Repeat until all the eggplant is cooked. Remember to allow the heat in the pan to recover before each batch is sautéed.

TO SERVE: Sprinkle each slice with chopped parsley and serve as required while hot.

For frying choose the long slim eggplants, they are a little dryer and will fry better. Eggplant should be sautéed in hot oil over a high heat to get the best results. Olive oil best enhances their flavour.

INGREDIENTS — SERVES 6

6–12	5mm ($^{1}/_{5}$″) slices of eggplant, depending on size
1	clove garlic, cut in half
	extra virgin olive oil
	ground pepper and salt
	chopped parsley

VEGETABLE SPAGHETTI

Vegetable spaghetti is made with long thin strips of carrot, courgette and sometimes leek. They may be served on their own with a light beurre fondue or as part of a main dish.

METHOD: Slice the carrots into thin strips, lengthways, then cut into long thin pieces. Repeat with the courgettes. Keep the two apart.

Make a quantity of beurre fondue, then put aside and keep just warm.

Bring a small pot of salted water to the boil. Blanch the carrot spaghetti until just limp. Remove from the heat and place in iced water. Quickly and carefully blanch the courgette then refresh in iced water, still keeping the two separate. Drain each well and ensure they are dry.

TO SERVE: Heat a little clarified butter in 2 sauté pans. Toss each vegetable spaghetti and warm through. Season each. Add beurre fondue and toss to evenly coat. Serve in tidy bundles, as required.

INGREDIENTS — SERVES 6–8

3	medium-sized carrots
3	medium-sized courgettes
	pepper and salt
	Beurre Fondue (see page 132)

BRAISED SHALLOTS

Shallots have a delicate flavour, much less pungent than regular onions. They are usually a small bulb, with a coppery coloured skin, and purple to mauve flesh. Shallots are excellent for flavouring delicate sauces such as beurre blanc.

METHOD: Peel the shallots, keeping them whole. Heat a little clarified butter in a large sauté pan. Add the shallots and toss over a high heat. Season and allow to begin to brown on the outside.

Place in an ovenproof dish, half cover with beef stock, and add the thyme. Bring to the boil on the stove top, then cover and cook in a preheated oven at 190–200°C (390°F) for 15 minutes, or until tender. Once cooked, remove from the stock and drain.

NOTE: The flavour of shallots can be further enhanced by tossing them in a little hot clear honey and very slightly caramelising just before serving.

INGREDIENTS — SERVES 6

12	evenly sized shallots
25g (1 oz)	clarified butter
	pepper and salt
150ml (⅔ cup)	Beef Stock (see page 140)
1	sprig thyme

SPINACH SUBRIC

A subric is a baked vegetable purée or mousse, to which herbs and spices, eggs and cream are added. The mixture is then poured into buttered dariole moulds and baked in the oven, set in a bain marie.

At Huka Lodge we make subric mainly from carrot, pumpkin, kumara, celeriac and spinach, but there are many more variations.

For all the above varieties the processes, and generally the quantities, are the same, although some purées may need more or less egg and cooling time.

INGREDIENTS — MAKES 6 x 100ML (½ CUP) MOULDS

500g	(1 lb)	raw spinach
250ml	(1 cup)	cream
1		small clove garlic, crushed
2		eggs
1		egg yolk
1		good pinch nutmeg pepper and salt

METHOD: Trim all the hard stalk and stem off the spinach, wash then blanch it in a little salted water until tender. Drain, refresh, then squeeze dry. Place the spinach, cream and garlic in a suitable pot. Place over medium heat and reduce the cream by half, or until it begins to get slightly thick. Remove from the heat and allow to cool. Place the spinach and cream in a liquidiser with 1 egg. Liquidise until very smooth, adding the remaining egg and yolk as you go. Pour into a clean bowl, season with nutmeg, pepper and salt.

THE TESTER: It is a good idea to test a small amount of any mousse you prepare. To do this place a little in a buttered mould and bake in the oven at 170° C (340° F) in a bain marie. Once cooked, turn out and test for firmness, seasoning and general taste.

Doing a 'tester' with your mousse gives you much more confidence when you come to serve it, as then you know your mousse will work. Add more cream if too hard, or egg if too soft, and correct the seasoning if necessary.

TO COOK: Preheat the oven to 170–180° C (340–350° F). Fill 6 chilled dariole moulds with melted clarified butter. Tip out the excess, leaving a complete layer of butter lining on the inside. Pour in the spinach mixture to within 4mm (¹/₈″) of the top of each mould. Butter small squares of tinfoil and cover each mould.

Place a small cloth in the bottom of a bain marie (use a roasting tray) and put in the subrics. Fill with hot water, two-thirds of the way up the moulds. Place in the oven and cook for approximately 20–25 minutes, or until firm.

Remove from the oven once cooked, allow to stand for 5–10 minutes on the bench top, then shake out onto serving plates. Serve while warm.

The ingredients for braising cabbage differ from white to red cabbage. With red cabbage everything from red wine to prunes may be added to enhance the flavour. However, braising green or white cabbage is generally less complicated.

INGREDIENTS — SERVES 6–8

500g	(1 lb)	green cabbage
200ml (1 small cup)		Chicken Stock (see page 138) or Vegetable Stock (see page 139)
25ml	(2 tbsp)	white wine vinegar
½ tsp		dried mixed herbs ground pepper and salt

BRAISED CABBAGE (WHITE)

METHOD: Remove the leaves from the cabbage, trying to keep them quite large. Trim off all heavy stalk and ribs. Wash in a little salted water.

Bring a small pot of salted water to the boil. Quickly blanch the cabbage leaves in batches until only just limp. Refresh in iced water.

When all the leaves are blanched, divide into 6–8 even portions, laying the leaves on top of each other. With the aid of a clean cloth form each into a ball. Twist tightly so each cabbage ball holds its shape.

Place the stock and vinegar in an ovenproof casserole; add the herbs. Quickly bring to the boil on the stove top, carefully add the cabbage balls, and sprinkle with pepper and salt. Cover and cook in a preheated oven at 200° C (400° F) for 10 minutes.

TO SERVE: Remove from the casserole, brush each ball with a little melted butter and serve as required.

GLAZED CARROTS AND BABY VEGETABLES

There are many ways to glaze carrots or baby vegetables. Firstly, what do we mean by 'glazing'? With reference to vegetables it refers to coating, say baby carrots, in a hot, shiny substance such as clarified or unsalted butter and sugar or honey just before serving. Carrots, plainly sliced, can be glazed by cooking them in water and butter over a high heat. The water completely evaporates, leaving only the butter. The carrots are further cooked and tossed in the remaining butter for a couple of minutes so they look rich and shiny.

Baby vegetables may be blanched first, then refreshed in iced water, drained and dried. When required, melt a little clarified butter in a large sauté pan. Add the baby vegetables, toss them until they are warmed through, then add unsalted butter or honey, season with pepper and salt, and serve immediately. This can be done with herb butters also. Be sure to toss the baby vegetables to ensure an even coating.

If adding anything such as chopped parsley to glazed carrots or turnips, add it at the end, toss to spread it through, then serve.

BUTTERS

Flavoured butters such as basil butter Maître d'Hôtel can be made in bulk, well covered and kept in the refrigerator for up to a week, or frozen in convenient quantities for up to 3 months.

Butter sauces such as Beurre Battu and Beurre Fondue are often beautiful with vegetables. Light, with delicate flavouring, these sauces are slightly difficult to make, but transform inexpensive vegetables into a remarkable eating experience. Always use unsalted butter so you can control seasoning.

METHOD: Beat the soft butter until smooth and creamy. Add the lemon juice and beat in. Add the chopped herbs and mix in. Season to taste.

TO STORE: Fill a piping bag fitted with a 2cm (¾") plain nozzle with herb butter. Pipe a row of butter the length of a conveniently sized piece of greaseproof paper. Roll up the paper, then twist each end to make a skinny cylinder. Place in the refrigerator or freeze.

TO USE: Heat a sauté pan or suitable pot over medium heat. Melt a little clarified butter then add blanched, drained and dried vegetables. Toss in the clarified butter until well heated through. Just before serving add the herb butter and toss through the vegetables until completely melted. You will require a dessertspoon of butter for 6 portions of fresh vegetables.

NOTE: Do not cook the vegetables in herb butter or it may burn.

Flavoured butters range from lobster flavoured, through every conceivable herb, to lemon. Once vegetables are blanched and ready for serving, they can be tossed in a variety of herb-flavoured butters or butter sauces. The butter keeps the vegetables hot and the flavouring is added at the same time.

HERB BUTTER — MAKES 500G (1 LB)

500g (1 lb)	unsalted butter, softened
	juice of 1 lemon
1 tbsp	fresh mixed herbs (basil, parsley, chervil, thyme) or all basil
	ground pepper and salt

BEURRES FONDUE AND BATTU

Beurre Fondue and Beurre Battu are similar in preparation and appearance, the idea being to melt butter without splitting it, producing a velvety butter sauce. Once prepared the butter may be kept warm in a bain marie, but if overheated just slightly, it will split. We find it best to use the butter as soon as it is made, tossing the already heated vegetables in the Beurre Fondue then serving.

The addition of a couple of drops of arrowroot, dissolved in water before the butter goes in, will hold the sauce together and make it much more durable. This is, however, regarded as cheating!

METHOD: Place the water in a heavy pot (non-reactive) and boil over high heat. Cut the butter into small cubes. Reduce the heat then add the butter, 2 pieces at a time, whisking vigorously until all the butter is incorporated.

Remove from the heat, whisk in the lemon juice then season to taste. Keep the sauce warm until used.

INGREDIENTS — MAKES ABOUT 200ML (1 SMALL CUP)

100ml (½ cup)	water
110g (4 oz)	cold unsalted butter
	juice of 1 lemon
	pinch of salt

POTATOES

There are many different types of potato; round to oval, white to pink. Everybody seems to like potatoes in some way, but there is a difference in the type of potato used for sauté or boiling, and mashing or baking.

Firm, all-purpose white or waxy potatoes are best for sautéing, frying or boiling whole, whereas dry, older and floury varieties are better for mashing or baking.

All potatoes generally keep best stored in a cool dark place away from the damp. If exposed to the light they may begin to sprout or develop green patches. According to the experts, these green patches and sprouts contain poisonous alkaloids and should be avoided or cut away.

There are hundreds of classic ways in which to serve the humble potato, from plain boiled to exotic dishes containing truffles and herbs. The following five variations are our favourites. Allow 1kg (2¼ lb) of old potatoes for 6 portions and 700–800g (1½–1¾ lb) new potatoes for 6 portions.

For this potato dish, again use firm, all-purpose potatoes — larger ones make the job easier and quicker. They should, however, be smooth and evenly shaped. These potatoes are best made the day before required.

INGREDIENTS — SERVES 6-8

700g	(1½ lb)	potatoes
10g	(½ oz)	butter for brushing tray
		grated nutmeg
1		large clove garlic
200ml		
(1 small cup)		cream
20g		grated parmesan or gruyère

For châteaux potatoes, choose small, evenly sized potatoes, firm and not old. Allow 2 per portion.

INGREDIENTS — SERVES 6

12		small, even potatoes
		salted water
		pepper and salt
		clarified butter

Classically, fondant potatoes are prepared the same way as châteaux potatoes: turned into barrel shapes and half covered with stock then baked in the oven with the aid of butter until all the stock is soaked up by the potatoes.

The following recipe is a variation of this concept. We find it easier, tastier and more interesting.

INGREDIENTS — SERVES 6

12		potato discs 1mm (½″) thick, cut with a 6cm (2″) plain cutter
50ml	(3½ tbsp)	melted clarified butter
100ml	(½ cup)	Brown Beef Stock (see page 140)
150g	(5 oz)	unsalted butter pepper and salt

GRATINED DAUPHINE POTATOES (GRATIN DE DAUPHINOISE)

METHOD: Wash and peel the potatoes. Thinly slice the potatoes and place in a large basin. Season with salt and pepper and a good pinch of nutmeg.

Well grease an ovenproof dish or small baking or roasting tray; rub the bottom and sides with garlic. Lay the sliced potatoes evenly in the tray or dish. Pour on the cream then sprinkle over the cheese. Place in a pre-heated oven at 170–180°C (340–350°F) for 40 to 45 minutes. Remove from the heat and allow to cool on the bench top; cover then place in the refrigerator to cool completely and set.

TO SERVE: Using a sharp knife, cut into even squares, lift out with a spatula or palette knife and place on a flat baking sheet. Place in a hot oven at 190°C (380°F) and reheat; making sure you heat right through. Remove from the heat and serve as required.

CHÂTEAUX POTATOES

METHOD: Wash and peel the potatoes. Turn into 8-sided barrel shapes, approx. 4cm (2″) long, and ranging from a 1.5cm (½″) diameter at each end to a 2.5cm (1″) diameter in the middle.

Bring plenty of salted water to the boil. Drop the potatoes in and blanch for 2–3 minutes. Drain and dry.

Melt plenty of clarified butter in a large sauté pan or roasting tray. Add the potatoes and lightly brown on all sides on the stove top. Season, then place in a hot oven at 200–230°C (400–450°F) for 20 minutes, turning regularly to ensure even cooking and colouring. Serve hot as required.

FONDANT POTATOES

METHOD: Melt the clarified butter in a large sauté pan over high heat. Add the prepared potato discs. Carefully add the beef stock then the butter. Season to taste.

Cook the potatoes over a medium to high heat; do not shake or move the potato discs in any way. Cook until the liquid turns clear and you can see the potatoes are browning around the bottom edges. Carefully turn with a palette knife. The discs should be golden brown in the centre with a dark brown ring around the rim.

Once turned over, finish in a preheated oven at 230°C (450°F) until tender. The butter left in the pan should be frothing during the final cooking stages.

Once cooked, transfer into a clean dish. Strain the remaining butter over the potatoes and keep warm until required.

To serve, shake off excess butter but do not dab dry, and serve as required.

PLAIN BOILED PARSLEY POTATOES

METHOD: Wash, scrub and peel the potatoes, and 'turn' if necessary. Bring plenty of salted water to the boil, drop the potatoes in and bring back to boil. Lower the heat and gently simmer for 10-20 minutes, or until tender. Test regularly with a small skewer. Drain once tender.

Melt the butter in a large pot or sauté pan. Toss the drained and dry potatoes in butter over a gentle to medium heat. Season with salt and pepper.

Just before serving, add chopped parsley and toss 2 or 3 times to evenly distribute. Serve while hot as required.

For these, choose small, firm, walnut-sized potatoes; all-purpose or waxy maincrop will do fine. If you have only large potatoes, they may be shaped into barrel shapes with a small vegetable knife (a process called 'turning').

INGREDIENTS — SERVES 6

	enough potatoes for 6 even portions
	salted water to cover
50g (2 oz)	unsalted butter
1 dsp	chopped parsley, washed and squeezed dry

MARQUISE POTATOES

METHOD: Wash and peel the potatoes, then cut into small even pieces. Cook in plenty of salted water until tender. Drain off all the water then place over a gentle heat for a few minutes, tossing occasionally to dry out. Mash until smooth, whipping with a fork to ensure all lumps are removed. Allow to cool a little.

Add the egg yolks and vigorously beat in; add the butter and mix in. Season with salt and pepper and add nutmeg.

Finely chop the blanched tomatoes and season with salt and pepper to taste. Mix in the chopped parsley.

Fill a piping bag fitted with a large star nozzle with the potato mixture. On a lightly buttered baking sheet pipe out 12 small nests about 1.5cm in diameter and 2.5cm high. Place in a hot oven for 3 minutes to harden the outside. Brush with egg-wash. Carefully fill each nest with tomato. Return to a hot oven or brown under the grill. Serve as required.

These are attractive, small nests of Duchesse potato filled with tomato concassé. We like to make them small and serve two per portion. Use older floury potatoes which are better for mashing.

INGREDIENTS

700g (1½ lb)	potato
2-3	egg yolks
50g (2 oz)	unsalted butter
	pepper and salt
	pinch of nutmeg
2	tomatoes, blanched, skinned and seeded
2 tsp	chopped parsley
1	egg, beaten with a little milk, for egg-wash

A farce or forcemeat is a delicate filling for meat dishes or a pâté. The French word 'farce' means practical joke, and has been applied to this type of preparation since the time it was common to play a joke on guests by filling a small animal with a different filling or 'farce'. It was much later that farces were improved to enhance the food they were in.

As the binding agent in the farce is the meat's natural protein and, in this recipe, egg white, it is essential to keep the ingredients chilled during all stages of preparation. Both these elements are extremely sensitive to heat and if they become too warm before cooking, they will coagulate and the farce will split and lose all its usefulness as a binding agent.

This recipe may be altered by simply changing the base meat to suit the animal or bird being used, i.e. pheasant instead of chicken in a pheasant dish. All other ingredients remain the same.

HUKA LODGE SAVOURY FARCE

INGREDIENTS — MAKES ABOUT 450G (1 LB)

300g (10 oz)	raw chicken or other similar meat, free of all bone and sinews	1 tsp	chopped mixed herbs
		30ml (2 tbsp)	brandy
		½ tsp	crushed garlic
		150ml (⅔ cup)	cream
2	egg whites		ground pepper and salt
1 tsp	chopped truffle (optional)		

METHOD: Chill all ingredients before use. Trim the meat. Blend it in a food processor until very smooth, adding the egg white as you go, or mince until very fine then beat the egg whites in over a bowl of ice. Push through a sieve to remove fibres, etc., and place the mixture in a clean bowl set in a larger bowl containing ice.

Add the herbs and the brandy and mix together well. Mix in the cream a little at a time until well incorporated. Season to taste with pepper and salt. Cover well with plastic wrap and leave in the refrigerator until ready to use. Due to the cream content this farce will keep only 24 hours.

The success of any dish depends to a great degree on the quality of the base product. To my mind, salad dressings are a good example of this. It is essential to use good oils, high quality vinegars, and fresh added ingredients where possible.

Always serve your vinaigrette at room temperature and try to make it well in advance to allow all the ingredients to marry together. Vinaigrettes keep well and improve with age.

HUKA LODGE HERB VINAIGRETTE

INGREDIENTS — SERVES 6

1	medium-sized shallot, thinly sliced into rings	2 tbsp (3 tbsp)	fresh picked herbs (chervil, parsley, marjoram)
1 tsp	wholegrain mustard	½ tbsp	finely chopped chives
½	clove garlic, crushed	150ml (⅔ cup)	virgin olive oil
		50ml (3½ tbsp)	walnut oil
3 tbsp (4 tbsp)	white wine vinegar		juice of 1 lemon
			ground pepper and salt

METHOD: Place the shallot, mustard, garlic, herbs and vinegar in a bowl. Pour on the oils, whisking as you go; add the lemon juice. Season with pepper and salt to taste. Allow to stand for 2 hours before use.

NOODLE DOUGH

METHOD: Add the salt to the flour and mix together. Beat the eggs and egg yolks together with the oil. Make a well in the flour and pour the egg mixture into the middle. Alternatively, steadily add to the flour in the electric mixer set on a low to medium setting. Incorporate flour until a thick mass is achieved.

Knead for 3–5 minutes, until the dough is very smooth. Cover and rest the dough for half an hour, out of the refrigerator.

ROLLING BY HAND: Once the dough has been mixed together, knead it with the palm of your hands for 3–5 minutes until the dough is very smooth. Use a little flour if it gets too sticky. Once kneaded, cover with a dry cloth and rest it in the refrigerator for half an hour. Roll out on a clean, dry and smooth work surface. Roll away from your body, turning and rolling as you go. Let the edge of the dough nearest to you hang over the edge of the bench as you roll and turn, thus causing the dough to stretch, aiding the rolling process. Roll out until the dough is so thin you can almost see through it. Allow to dry for 10–15 minutes before cutting it. Carefully turn the dough a couple of times during the drying process.

CUTTING BY HAND: For the production of pasta shapes such as ravioli or farfalle, a hand-operated fluted pastry wheel is good for cutting. For noodles such as tagliatelle or tagliarini, roll up the dried sheet of pasta into quite a tight roll, then slice across at 4–5mm ($^{1}/_{6}$″) intervals for tagliatelle and 2mm ($^{1}/_{10}$″) intervals for tagliarini. Unroll dough and lay flat on a lightly floured tray or hang it over a broom handle between 2 chairs.

ROLLING BY PASTA MACHINE: At Huka Lodge we have a small benchtop, hand-operated pasta machine. It was relatively inexpensive, and the work it saves without affecting quality makes it worth thousands.

Once the dough has been mixed and kneaded as before, let it rest for 30 minutes then cut it into 4–6 pieces. Lightly dust with flour and feed into the rollers set at their widest adjustment. Lightly dust with flour again. Close the roller adjustment to halfway between the thickest and thinnest settings, and feed through again. Dust again if necessary, set the rollers on their finest setting, and feed the pasta through a third time. Repeat the process with the remaining dough. If making noodles such as tagliatelle or tagliarini, allow the strips of dough to dry slightly on the bench for 15 minutes before cutting. If making other pasta shapes or ravioli, use straight away.

TO COOK PASTA AND NOODLES: Cook in plenty of well-salted water with a knob of butter or 2 tablespoons of cooking oil for 3–4 minutes for fresh pasta, longer for dried pasta. Keep a close eye on it during cooking and keep moving it slightly to prevent the pasta sticking together.

We use the following noodle dough recipe as a base for almost all our pasta dishes. Its easy preparation and readiness to accept a wide variety of flavourings makes it a necessity in any kitchen.

There are, however, several points about making and cooking pasta that should be noted.

The actual production of the dough is quite simple and may be done by hand or with an electric mixer. If preparing the dough by hand, keep your left hand dry and mix with your right hand, carefully and gradually adding flour with your left hand until you have a thick mass ready for kneading. Keep adding flour until you end up with a moist, pliable dough, not a sticky dough.

When making the dough in an electric mixer, use a dough hook and have the machine on low to medium. Once all ingredients are blended, remove from the machine and continue to knead by hand.

INGREDIENTS
— MAKES 500G (1 LB)

500g	(1 lb)	standard flour
10g	(½ oz)	salt
4		whole eggs
6		egg yolks
2 tsp		walnut oil (or olive oil)

To my mind, stocks form the basis of successful cooking. Without them any degree of flavour cannot be achieved. They are the foundation of all our sauces, soups, savoury jellies and poaching liquids.

There is really no excuse for not having a supply of base stocks as they are inexpensive to make, require only basic skills and knowledge in their preparation, and will keep for up to five days well chilled and covered in the fridge. They may also be frozen in convenient quantities and will keep for weeks.

A stock pot is not a 'leftovers' container into which everything is thrown. Follow correct procedures, use good wholesome ingredients and take care in their preparation — these are the key to your success.

Chicken stock is the stock used most in our kitchen. It is used as a base to many of the cold entrées, soups and sauces.

Once made, a chicken stock will keep up to a week if well chilled and covered to prevent it from absorbing other fridge smells. If frozen, it will keep up to one month.

As with all good stocks, chicken stock should lightly gel when cold.

The best chicken stock is made by using the whole bird — preferably a 'boiling fowl'. This can be quite expensive, so most chefs use chicken carcasses, wings and neck.

STOCKS

During the cooking process of all stocks you must skim off any impurities as they rise to the surface. If not, they will boil into the liquid and make your stock cloudy.

Once your stock has reached the boil, lower the heat and simmer for the stipulated time. Never boil hard for extended periods of time and don't allow the level of liquid to drop below the level of solid ingredients or once again your stock will become cloudy.

Always use chicken for chicken stock, beef or veal for beef or veal stock and so on. Try not to mix base ingredients or you won't be able to achieve a pronounced flavour. Game stock is the only exception.

As a stock takes some time to cook, it is not advisable to cut any of the vegetables you add into small pieces. They will turn mushy and cloud the stock, and reabsorb some of the flavours. Wash them well, and where possible leave them whole. Add them after the stock has boiled and has been skimmed.

CHICKEN STOCK (WHITE)

INGREDIENTS
— MAKES ABOUT 2 LITRES (3½ PINTS)

1	no.9 chicken or 1.5kg (3⅓ lb) chicken carcass, wings and neck bone	1	medium-sized bayleaf
		1	clove
		4	stalks parsley
100g (4 oz)	white of leek	6	white peppercorns
100g (4 oz)	celery		
100g (4 oz)	carrot	1	sprig thyme
1	medium-sized onion	2.5 litres (4½ pints)	cold water

METHOD: Wash any excess blood from the chicken or bones. Wash and peel all the vegetables, and stud the onion with the clove and bayleaf. Place all the ingredients, apart from the vegetables, in a large pot and cover with the cold water.

Bring to the boil, skimming as necessary. Once boiled, add the vegetables, lower the heat to a gentle simmer and continue cooking for 1½– 2 hours, skimming as necessary. There should be 1.8 litres (3 pints) of stock after 1½ hours.

Remove from the heat, and pass through a fine sieve lined with a clean muslin cloth into a suitable container. Allow to cool slightly before placing in the fridge.

For turkey stock, follow the same procedure but substitute turkey bones for the chicken bones.

NOTE: Chill stock in the refrigerator overnight, then the next day remove all the solidified fat which has formed on the top. The same applies to all other stocks as well. If you are freezing your stock, do this first.

VEGETABLE STOCK

INGREDIENTS — MAKES 600ML (1 PINT)

25g (1 oz)	unsalted butter	1	sprig thyme
1	medium-sized onion	1	sprig chervil
70g (3 oz)	celery	2	stalks parsley
50g (2 oz)	white of leek	4	white peppercorns
1	small clove garlic	1	small bayleaf
1	medium-sized carrot	1 litre (4½ cups)	cold water
2	ripe tomatoes		

METHOD: Melt the butter in a large pot, add the next 5 ingredients and sweat without colouring. Pour on water. Bring to the boil, skimming when required. Lower the heat and gently simmer for 10 minutes. Add all the remaining ingredients and continue to simmer for a further 10 minutes. Pass into a clean pot then reduce to about 600ml (1 pint) over medium heat. Remove from the heat and cool. Store in the refrigerator or freeze.

A great deal of care must be taken in the preparation of a vegetable stock to ensure clarity and taste.

The addition of tomatoes will ensure a clear stock is achieved, and reducing the stock once the vegetables have been removed will enhance the flavour.

This too is a useful stock in the preparation of soups, sauces and aspics.

FISH STOCK

INGREDIENTS — MAKES ABOUT 1 LITRE (1¾ PINTS)

1 kg (2¼ lb)	fish bones and trimmings
500ml (2¼ cups)	water
500ml (2¼ cups)	dry white wine
1	bayleaf
4	white peppercorns
25g (1 oz)	chopped leek
1	medium-sized onion, chopped
25g (1 oz)	celery
1	stalk parsley

METHOD: Roughly chop the bones. Place in a large pot and pour over the water and wine. Bring to the boil over a gentle heat, skimming off any impurities as they rise.

Add the vegetables and herbs. Simmer for 20 minutes. Pass through a fine sieve into a clean container.

This stock may be used as is, or reduced by half to concentrate the flavour. Allow to cool, and store in the refrigerator.

The best fish bones to use for fish stock are snapper, sole or flounder. It is very important that you do not overcook fish stock or it will become bitter and cloudy. Make absolutely certain all your ingredients are very clean. Wash and trim off any blood or roe.

BROWN GAME STOCK

INGREDIENTS — MAKES ABOUT 1 LITRE (1¾ PINTS)

1 kg (2¼ lb)	game trimmings carcass, necks	250ml (1 cup)		full-bodied red wine
10ml (2 tsp)	grapeseed or walnut oil (not olive)	500ml (2¼ cups)		Veal Stock (see below)
		1 litre (4½ cups)		cold water
1	medium-sized onion	1		sprig sage
		1		sprig thyme
1	medium-sized carrot	2		stalks parsley
		6		black peppercorns
50g (2 oz)	celery	1		bayleaf
250ml (1 cup)	madeira	6		juniper berries

METHOD: Chop all the bones and meat. Pour the oil into a roasting tray and heat over a high flame on the stove top. Add the bones and meat and brown on all sides.

Wash and peel the vegetables, cut into large pieces, and add to the bones. Continue to cook for 5 minutes, then add the red wine and madeira. Bring to the boil, lower the heat and simmer 10 minutes.

Pour into a large pot and add the veal stock and water. Place over a high heat and bring to the boil, skimming off the impurities as they rise. Lower the heat to a gentle simmer then add the herbs. Continue to simmer gently for 2 hours. Once cooked, pass through a fine sieve lined with a muslin cloth into a suitable container. Allow to cool, and place in the refrigerator.

BROWN VEAL STOCK

INGREDIENTS — MAKES ABOUT 1 LITRE (1¾ PINTS)

1 kg (2¼ lb)	veal knuckles and marrow bones or beef bones	4		ripe tomatoes
		1		clove garlic, crushed
75g (3 oz)	mushroom trimmings	2		stalks parsley
		1		bayleaf
100g (4 oz)	carrot	1		sprig thyme
50g (2 oz)	onion	2.5 litres (4½ pints)		cold water
50g (2 oz)	celery	5		black peppercorns
50g (2 oz)	white of leek			

METHOD: Heat the oven to 200°C (400°F). Roughly chop the vegetables, or leave whole. Roast the bones in the oven until well browned. Remove from the heat and place in a large pot. Place the roasting tray over medium heat on the stove top, add the garlic and vegetables, and lightly brown. Place the vegetables aside until required. Deglaze the roasting tray by adding a little water.

This stock is made with game trimmings and bones. Most types of game birds are suitable — pheasant, quail, pigeon — along with rabbit and hare. To make brown duck stock follow exactly the same process as for game stock, using duck bones only. The same applies for making pheasant stock.

I personally find a better stock is achieved without the use of venison bones and trimmings. If I require venison stock, again, I follow the same process as for game stock, using only venison bones and trimmings.

Veal stock, made from veal knuckles and marrow bones roasted in the oven, results in a great stock and even greater sauces once refined further.

Beef bones may be used, following the same process as for veal stock, but often the result is an overpowering and sometimes greasy stock.

This stock may be used to make many sauces, including demi-glaze, as well as soups and aspics.

Pour cold water over the bones then bring to the boil over a high heat, skimming off all impurities throughout the cooking process. Once boiled, lower the heat to a gentle simmer. Cook for one hour then add all the vegetables and herbs. Continue cooking for 2–2½ hours, skimming when needed. Top up with cold water if necessary, i.e. if the liquid drops below the level of the solid ingredients.

Once cooked, remove from the heat and pass through a fine sieve lined with muslin into a suitable container. Allow to cool, then cover and store in the refrigerator.

DEMI-GLAZE

Classically, demi-glaze, or 'demi' as it is sometimes referred to, is equal quantities of brown sauce (espagnole) and brown stock mixed together then reduced by half. This is a long process involving 3 separate procedures; making the stock, making the brown sauce, and making the actual demi. Consequently, many variations have developed, some good and some not so good.

There is also some variation of opinion as to exactly what demi-glaze is; while some stick to the classical, others consider well-reduced veal stock to be demi-glaze.

I take the middle ground, and consider the addition of red wine, madeira, herbs and vegetables to play a large part in its success.

The beauty of this recipe is that it may be prepared in quantity and stored covered and well chilled. It can be used as a base for many sauces, changing the flavour to suit by infusing the roasted or browned bones of the relevant meat. This recipe may be doubled quite safely.

INGREDIENTS — MAKES 600ML (1 PINT)

2 litres (3½ pints)	Veal (or Beef) Stock (see page 140)	75g (3 oz)	dried herbs
		1	medium-sized onion, sliced
300ml (1¼ cups)	madeira	2	medium-sized carrots, chopped
350ml (1½ cups)	red wine		
100g (4 oz)	mushroom trimmings	100g (4 oz)	celery, chopped
		2 tsp	ground pepper
1 tbsp	tomato paste		

METHOD: Place the first 6 ingredients together in a large pot over high heat and reduce by one-third. Add all the remaining ingredients, lower the heat, and gently simmer until the liquid has reduced by another third. Remove from the heat and pass through a fine sieve lined with damp muslin into a suitable container. Allow to cool, cover, then store in the refrigerator.

BRIOCHE

Freshly baked brioche is easily my favourite bread: rich and buttery yet so light.

At Huka Lodge we make the small, individual buns baked in the traditional fluted brioche moulds. We also make brioche loaves, which are used for slicing and toasting or for croûtons. The leftover pieces are made into crumbs for coating and herb crusts.

Making the brioche is quite a long process, due mainly to proving or rising times. However, brioche freezes well once baked; you may make and freeze a good supply. The following recipe yields about 1.8kg (4 lb) of dough.

Brioche dough may be made the night before baking, well covered, and kept in the refrigerator.

METHOD: Sift the flour into a mixing bowl; mix in the sugar and salt. Combine the milk and water and warm to blood temperature. Add the yeast and completely dissolve in the milk.

Using a dough hook attachment and the electric mixer set at a slow to medium speed, mix in the eggs one by one. Pour in the yeast and milk mixture. Continue to mix for 3–5 minutes, until the dough is smooth.

Cut the soft butter into small knobs and add to the dough one by one, mixing at a steady speed. Once all the butter is in, continue to mix for a further 3 minutes. By now the dough should be smooth and elastic.

Cover the bowl with a clean teatowel and place in the refrigerator for 2 hours. The dough will rise but not too much. Tip out onto a lightly floured work surface and knead a second time by hand for 2 minutes.

INGREDIENTS
MAKES ABOUT 1.8KG (4 LB) DOUGH

900g	(2 lb)	standard flour
75g	(3 oz)	castor sugar
2½ tsp		salt
75ml	(⅓ cup)	milk, warmed
75ml	(⅓ cup)	water, warmed
40g	(1½ oz)	fresh yeast
8		eggs
225g	(8 oz)	soft butter
		flour for dusting work surface and moulds
		butter for greasing moulds
		egg yolks beaten with a little milk for glazing.

INDIVIDUAL BRIOCHE BUNS

METHOD: Cut off pieces of dough weighing about 50g (2 oz) each, then cut a quarter off each piece. Roll each into a ball using the palm of your hand and dusting with flour. Place the larger ball in a well-buttered and lightly dusted brioche mould. Make an indentation in it with your thumb then place the small ball on top. Press together lightly so they don't separate when cooking.

Allow to prove (rise) at room temperature until double in size. Carefully glaze with egg and milk mixture. Place in a preheated oven at 230° C (450° F) for 10–15 minutes.

Once baked, remove from the moulds and allow to cool on wire racks. If freezing, cover well and place in the freezer in convenient quantities.

BRIOCHE LOAVES

METHOD: Evenly divide the dough into 3 pieces, then cut each into 3 again. Butter and dust 3 loaf tins (25 x 10cm; 10″ x 4″).

Roll each piece into a smooth, even ball and place 3 balls in each tin. Prove at room temperature until double in size. Carefully brush with egg yolk and milk mixture.

Cook in a hot, preheated oven at 200° C (400° F) for 30–40 minutes. Once baked, allow to cool a little then carefully remove from the tins. Cool on racks. Cover with plastic wrap if freezing.

PUFF PASTRY

The actual preparation of puff pastry is not difficult, but it does take some time to complete. This is due to the amount of resting time required between each turn.

With this in mind, the following recipe is for quite a large quantity as, once made, puff pastry freezes very well. A good stock can therefore be kept on hand, saving you from going through the long process each time you need the pastry. These quantities may be halved if preferred.

Take time in your preparation, as a good deal of care is required to ensure a light, flaky result.

INGREDIENTS
— MAKES ABOUT 2.5 KG (5½ LB)

1 kg	(2¼ lb)	standard flour
25g	(1 oz)	salt
500ml	(2¼ cups)	water
50ml	(3½ tbsp)	dry white wine
150g	(5 oz)	melted butter
800g	(1¾ lb)	softened butter (not too soft)
		flour for dusting

DOUGH: Place the flour in the bowl of your electric mixer; add the salt. Using a dough hook, and with the machine on a slow to medium speed, add the water and wine. Slowly pour in the melted butter. Continue to mix until well incorporated. Place on a lightly dusted work surface and knead by hand until smooth.

Roll into a ball. Cut a cross across the top of the ball of the dough to release the elasticity. Cover with a clean teatowel and rest it for 1 hour in the refrigerator.

Cut up the softened butter, sprinkle with a little flour and work it until it is the same consistency as the dough. Do not oversoften.

Roll the dough out to 60cm (24″) long and 40cm (16″) wide.

Roll the butter to 35cm (14″) long and 30cm (12″) wide.

Place the butter in the centre of the rolled out dough; lightly brush the edge of the dough with water. Fold both ends of the dough over the butter, press down the edges and any overlap firmly to seal in the butter. This will prevent any butter oozing out during the rolling and folding. Rest the dough in the refrigerator for 14 minutes.

FIRST TURN – 1 SINGLE FOLD: Roll the dough and butter out to their original size. Keep the pressure even when rolling and roll lengthways up and down.

Fold one-third of the pastry over so one end is folded into the centre. Now fold the remaining third over the top. You will have 3 layers. Keep the edges straight at all times. Using your thumb, make a small indentation in the dough so you can remember how many folds you have made as you go. Place in the refrigerator for 20 minutes.

SECOND TURN – 1 SINGLE FOLD: Place the pastry rectangle on a lightly floured work surface. Rotate the rectangle half a cycle from its original position, then repeat the above process exactly. Rest the pastry in the refrigerator for 25 minutes.

THIRD TURN – 1 DOUBLE FOLD: Place the pastry on a lightly floured surface; rotate the rectangle half a cycle from its last position. Once again roll the pastry out to its original size. Fold each end over so the ends meet evenly in the centre, then fold one half over the other. You will have 4 layers of pastry. Rest it in the refrigerator for 25 minutes.

FOURTH TURN – 1 DOUBLE FOLD: Place the pastry on a lightly floured work surface; rotate once again, half a cycle from its previous position.

Repeat the above double-turn process exactly.
Rest the pastry in the refrigerator for a further 25 minutes.

The puff pastry is now ready to use. When you roll out the pastry to use it, you will be rolling out the fourth turn. If you are freezing your puff pastry, cut it into conveniently sized pieces, cover well in plastic wrap, and store in the freezer. Always allow it to thaw naturally.

PÂTE SABLÉE
(SWEET SHORTBREAD PASTRY)

Like any pastry with a high butter and egg content, sable must not be overkneaded or it will become greasy and elastic. Too much handling will damage the pastry as the heat and oils from your hands will begin to break down the very delicate structure of the sable.

Well covered, sable will keep a week in the refrigerator, but it does not freeze very well.

Store in conveniently sized pieces or rolled into a cylinder; because of the high butter content it will become quite hard in the refrigerator.

METHOD: Cut the butter into small pieces, place in a bowl and work with your fingers until soft.

Sift the icing sugar then mix it into the butter along with a pinch of salt. Carefully add the egg yolks and mix well.

A little at a time, mix in the flour until it is all incorporated. Place on a lightly dusted work surface and knead with your hand 3 or 4 times only. Roll into a cylinder, wrap in plastic wrap and store in the refrigerator.

If you are going to use the pastry the same day, allow it to rest in the refrigerator at least 1 hour before using.

NOTE: When using pâte sablée, be quick when rolling and lining flans, etc., as the pastry softens quickly and becomes very hard to handle.

Sable is the French word for sand, an adequate resemblance to this delicate, light and crumbly pastry. Sable is superb as a crust for lemon tarts or served as little biscuits with fresh berries such as the famous 'Sable aux Fraises' by the Roux brothers.

INGREDIENTS

200g (7 oz)	soft, unsalted butter
100g (4 oz)	icing sugar
	pinch of salt
2	egg yolks
250g (9 oz)	standard flour

SHORT PASTRY

METHOD: Place the sifted flour in a large bowl, cut the butter into small pieces, then, using your fingertips, rub in the butter until a loose, sandy texture is achieved.

Mix together the egg, milk, sugar and salt, and lightly beat.

Make a well in the flour and pour in the egg mixture. Gradually mix the two. Once incorporated place on a lightly dusted work surface and knead 3 or 4 times. Cover with a clean cloth and place in the refrigerator to rest for 1½ hours before using. Alternatively, wrap in foil or plastic wrap in conveniently sized pieces and freeze.

Short pastry is very versatile, and may be used in many sweet and savoury dishes. It is light and crumbly and is good for fruit flans and some meat dishes. Once made and well covered, it will keep several days in the refrigerator. Short pastry will keep up to 3 months frozen.

INGREDIENTS
— MAKES ABOUT 450G (1 LB)

250g (9 oz)	standard flour
140g (5 oz)	unsalted butter (slightly soft)
1	egg
2 tsp	milk
1 tsp	icing sugar
	pinch of salt

SUGAR SYRUP

INGREDIENTS
— MAKES ABOUT 1 LITRE (1¾ PINTS)

600g (1¼ lb)	sugar
600ml (1 pint)	water
	juice of 2 limes

It is always useful to have sugar syrup on hand. It stores very well and, if covered, will keep in the refrigerator for some time. Sugar syrup is an all-purpose syrup, useful for brushing sweet terrines and gateaux, sorbets, ices and sweet sauces and coulis.

METHOD: Boil the sugar and water together for 1 minute. Add the lime juice.

Once cooked, pass through a fine sieve into a clean container. Allow to cool, then store in the refrigerator.

CRÈME FRAÎCHE

INGREDIENTS
MAKES ABOUT 500ML (2¼ CUPS)

450ml (2 cups)	full cream, at room temperature
4 tbsp (5 tbsp)	buttermilk

Although crème fraîche is commercially available, usually through a good cheese producer, there is, as with most things, a certain satisfaction in making your own.

Crème fraîche is delicious in soups, either mixed in or as a dollop on top. It may be used in savoury dips with herbs and cream cheese, and it may also be used in cream desserts instead of regular cream, such as yoghurt desserts or some bavarois.

METHOD: Add the buttermilk to the cream in a slightly warmed bowl. Cover securely and keep at 70–80°C (160–175°F) for 8–10 hours, allowing the mixture to thicken.

Once done, refrigerate and use as required. Crème fraîche will keep for 1–2 weeks.

GLOSSARY

AL DENTE: Refers to the cooking of fresh vegetables to a crisp stage.

BAIN MARIE: Water bath.

BLIND BAKING: To cook an empty pastry flan case without colouring.

BLANCH: Plunge into boiling water, to enhance colour and slightly cook. Also kills enzymes in fruit and vegetables which cause them to rot.

CHOCOLATE RUNOUTS: Chocolate designs piped onto greaseproof paper. Once hardened, removed and placed on desserts for garnish.

COATING CONSISTENCY: The stage when a sauce or custard is cooked to a degree that it will evenly coat the back of a spoon.

DARIOLE MOULD: Metal mould used in the production of some savoury and sweet mousses.

DEMOULD OR TURN OUT: Tip a mould or terrine from its mould.

FARCE: Savoury filling or forcemeat bound by the protein of the meat used and egg white.

FLASH: Brown under a fierce grill or salamander.

FLEURONS: Puff pastry crescents.

JUS: Highly flavoured juice from meats etc., refined and served as an accompanying sauce.

PASS: Pour a sauce or syrup through a sieve to remove solid ingredients.

REDUCE: Boil over high heat to reduce volume and increase flavour.

REFRESH: Plunge into iced water.

REST: Allow to sit in a warm place, usually covered, after removing from the oven; allow excess heat to decline.

RIBBON STAGE: Refers to the stage when a sabayon has been beaten over a bain marie until the whisk leaves definite tracks in the mixture.

ROUX: Equal quantities of flour and butter used to thicken soups and sauces.

SEAL: Cook meat on all sides on the stove top, to increase flavour.

SKIM: Remove fat and impurities from the top of soups, sauces and stocks.

SORBETIÈRE: Sorbet or ice cream machine.

SWEAT: Cook in butter with the lid on, without allowing to colour, e.g., onions.

RELAIS &
CHATEAUX